"Amy Vatne Bintliff has written a compelling description of the application of service learning and restorative principles, underscoring educational theory with the voices of youth and her fellow teachers. She provides ample evidence that the use of Circle in the curriculum, as a way to teach as well as to address conflict or harm, enhanced the educational process. More importantly, Circle helped the students and their teachers connect personally and professionally, providing for many of the students a safe and supportive learning environment such as they had never before experienced. The book is a great read, as Vatne Bintliff combines theory and story in a persuasive and clear way."

—Nancy Riestenberg, Prevention Specialist,
Minnesota Department of Education

"This book is an inspiring exploration of how teachers can build relationships with students that foster intellectual awakening and emotional growth. Disconnection and disengagement are all too common experiences, especially among marginalized and disadvantaged students. Amy Vatne Bintliff lovingly narrates a holistic journey of transformative education that deeply touches both students and teachers. The book offers a powerful illustration of the practical use of Circles in the student-teacher relationship. Vatne Bintliff's honest and penetrating reflections offer insight and guidance to teachers as they struggle to be emotionally aware and present with students. Above all, this book reminds us that a sense of community, trust, and connection are an essential foundation for a social justice curriculum."

—Carolyn Boyes-Watson, Professor of Sociology and Director
of the Center for Restorative Justice, Suffolk University;
Author of Peacemaking Circles and Urban Youth

"Stories connect us, and this compelling story delivers insight into the power of relationships, reflection, and generative questions.

In the NCLB world of tests and accountability we have forgotten the human connections and the mystery of learning that is at the heart of real teaching and learning. This book is a reminder of the potent learning that occurs when we focus on building a safe, supportive, challenging community.

Many schools talk about transformational learning, but this powerful story gives specific examples of transformation in action. The three R's of reflections, relationships, and relativity provide glimpses of the way community and caring create powerful learning opportunities.

Learning can't be compartmentalized—we learn through our emotions, our intellect, and our souls. We teach the whole person."

—Ron Petrich, Education Professor, Courage to Teach Facilitator,
Augsburg College, Minneapolis, Minnesota

RE-ENGAGING DISCONNECTED YOUTH

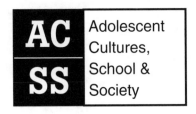

AC
SS
Adolescent
Cultures,
School &
Society

Joseph L. DeVitis & Linda Irwin-DeVitis
GENERAL EDITORS

Vol. 51

The Adolescent Cultures, School & Society series
is part of the Peter Lang Education list.
Every volume is peer reviewed and meets
the highest quality standards for content and production.

PETER LANG
New York • Washington, D.C./Baltimore • Bern
Frankfurt • Berlin • Brussels • Vienna • Oxford

Amy Vatne Bintliff

RE-ENGAGING
DISCONNECTED
YOUTH

*Transformative Learning
through Restorative and
Social Justice Education*

PETER LANG
New York • Washington, D.C./Baltimore • Bern
Frankfurt • Berlin • Brussels • Vienna • Oxford

Library of Congress Cataloging-in-Publication Data
Bintliff, Amy Vatne.
Re-engaging disconnected youth: transformative learning
through restorative and social justice education / Amy Vatne Bintliff.
p. cm. — (Adolescent cultures, school and society; v. 51)
Includes bibliographical references and index.
1. Alternative education—Minnesota—Case studies.
2. Outdoor education—Minnesota—Case studies. 3. Experiential learning—
Minnesota—Case studies. 4. Motivation in education—Minnesota—
Case studies. 5. Summer schools—Minnesota—Case studies.
6. Social justice—Study and teaching (Secondary)—Minnesota—
Case studies. 7. United States—Territorial expansion—
Study and teaching (Secondary) I. Title.
LC46.5.M6B56   371.0409776—dc22   2010046189
ISBN 978-1-4331-1005-4 (hardcover)
ISBN 978-1-4331-1004-7 (paperback)
ISSN 1091-1464

Bibliographic information published by **Die Deutsche Nationalbibliothek**.
Die Deutsche Nationalbibliothek lists this publication in the "Deutsche
Nationalbibliografie"; detailed bibliographic data is available
on the Internet at http://dnb.d-nb.de/.

Mixed Sources
Product group from well-managed
forests, controlled sources and
recycled wood or fiber
www.fsc.org   Cert no. SCS-COC-002464
©1996 Forest Stewardship Council

Cover photo by Amy Vatne Bintliff

The paper in this book meets the guidelines for permanence and durability
of the Committee on Production Guidelines for Book Longevity
of the Council of Library Resources.

© 2011 Peter Lang Publishing, Inc., New York
29 Broadway, 18th floor, New York, NY 10006
www.peterlang.com

Printed in the United States of America

For my Westward Bound students, your voices spoke eloquently.
Your trust inspired.

Table of Contents

Acknowledgments

I would first like to thank my Westward Bound students. You all shared so much with me both during the program and during the writing of this book. I grew as an educator and human being through our shared experiences and by listening to your voices speak honestly about your lives. I love you all.

To my dear colleagues, Angel Salathe and Randy Bauer, I owe my gratitude. The collaborative relationships that we have are simply filled with joy, creativity, and passion. Angel, even though miles now separate us, we will continue to partner to create great programs for students. Thank you for your words, insights, and encouragement during this long process. Randy, we miss you. Our community still grieves over the loss of a true environmentalist and passionate educator. I am so grateful that we got to share in those last interviews.

Thank you to the staff and leaders at the alternative school where this project took place. Your support and creativity is amazing!

To Kathy Seipp and the staff at The Advocates for Human Rights—thank you for your time, interviews, and the training that you provide for so many teachers. Your support continues to inspire me. Your organization was the voice that said, "Of course you can…"

To my Hamline professors, Walter Enloe and Paul Gorski, I owe a huge thanks. Your passion for social justice was contagious and your feedback helped greatly with the first drafts of Chapter Three.

To Dr. Carolyn-Boyes Watson for her inspiring Circle work.

To my editor, Joseph DeVitis. Your gentle encouragement, patience and feedback helped form this book. Thank you for believing that a classroom teacher can participate in the research community. So many teachers' voices are silenced in this practice—your work encourages new voices to emerge and that is much appreciated.

To the amazing staff at Peter Lang. Thank you for your expertise and quick responses.

And thanks finally to my husband, Chris, and daughter, Dakota Dawn, for your patience and encouragement. You set aside time for me to journey with my students, write, and research. You understand that teaching is a calling. Thank you.

CHAPTER ONE

Introduction:
Program Design and Implementation

I'm probably not the only one, but up until not that long ago, no one really saw me. No one got to know me. No one gave a crap who I was or what I was about. Anything. But, in the past year, I've met some of the most amazing people and I've connected with more people then I ever thought I would have. And I never thought I would trust to tell people the things that I have. Especially this group. It's hard to talk about the things that hurt you most, but we talk about it and I finally feel that I'm not so alone. Everybody's unique, but everybody's so much the same. It's nice to figure that out. To find that connection.

— Hannah, Westward Bound Summer School Student, 2006

This student and twenty-eight others, whose names have been changed to honor privacy, all shared in an experiential education summer school program that was designed and implemented at an alternative school in Minnesota. Students were offered credit in history, English, and science via a course that included an in-depth look at Westward Expansion history. During the three- to four-week course, students traveled from Minnesota to Wyoming stopping at historical sites along the way. The course, which included using restorative justice Talking Circles, hands-on learning, and curriculum that centered on human rights and social justice was designed by two other teachers and I because we saw that our students needed to reconnect with learning, with other individuals, and with their communities. Having worked with youth labeled "at-risk" for seven years, I had seen the fall-out of disconnections and loneliness. Drugs, alcohol, neglect, abuse, distrust, violence, criminal activities, truancy, disengagement with school, and feelings of alienation appeared time and time again at my alternative school. Over the course of three summers, 29 students experienced the program. Through qualitative interviews with both students and teachers, and the analyses of journals, it is evident that students experienced transformations in their ideas about race, culture, and historical events, their ideas about relating to others, and their actions and responses towards education.

A History of the Experiential Outdoor Education Program

In order to begin the discussion of what our students learned and what transformational learning occurred it is important to have background knowledge about the program as a whole. Over a four-year period of time, Angel Salathe, Randy Bauer, and I planned a unique learning experience for our alternative high school students. We believed that our students could succeed in school if they had more opportunities to have hands-on learning experiences both inside and outside of our building. We agreed with Herdman (1994) who wrote of Outward Bound experiences at a school in New York State:

> Our work with Outward Bound has been called experience-based or experiential education. To some, these terms mean simply learning by doing, but at George Washington we used physical experiences not only to bring students' academic class work to life, but also as a bridge to a greater understanding of their own lives. (p. 16)

We differed from Outward Bound in some elements, but we did want to foster the following design principles of expeditionary learning Outward Bound:

- The Primacy of Self-Discovery
- The Having of Wonderful Ideas
- The Responsibility of Learning
- Intimacy and Caring
- Collaboration
- Diversity
- The Natural World
- Solitude and Reflection
- Service and Compassion (Rugen and Hartl, 1994, pp. 20–21)

Although not an Outward Bound program, we wanted to focus on using nature, camping, and history to motivate disengaged youth. For many of our students, the stigma of "failure" in mainstream programs had adversely affected their desire to learn. Many students had been referred to an alternative education site due to truancy, failure to complete work, and a general "lack of motivation." We began asking students questions, such as, "Would you ever want to actually see the places you read about in history class?" and "Have you ever been camping before? Would you like to try it?" Many students expressed interest and we began planning.

Once funding was gathered from donors, Angel, a history teacher, and Randy, a science teacher, worked with me, an English teacher, to write summer school programming that included an outdoor education travel experience. The first summer, 2003, Angel and I laid the framework for an experiential study of the Lewis and Clark Trail. Students studied topics of history, social justice regarding the Native American perspective, and environmental preservation during a six-week classroom experience. We then left for an eight-day trip that followed the Lewis and Clark Trail as far as the Rocky Mountains. Leaving from Minnesota, we traveled through South Dakota, North Dakota, Montana, and Wyoming. As instructors during this experience, we observed higher student participation, more detailed journals and more positive group dynamics than in our traditional classes. We also noticed strong bonds forming within our group. Of those eight students, six graduated from high school, three went on to college, one dropped out of school, and one, sadly, died of an overdose.

The second summer, 2004, Angel and I asked Randy to join us. We studied the Oregon Trail in a similar manner, but we added science curriculum. Nine out of eleven of our students that year had expressed ideas about dropping out, many were addicted to drugs, and two were involved in gang activity. Each year we asked students to fill out an application asking why they wanted to go on this trip, and that year we admittedly recruited our students most at-risk of dropping out—our Hmong boys and Native American girls. They all filled out an application. In their application, some students said that they wanted to participate because they had never left the city and felt that they would only live for a short while and wanted to experience something new. Others said that the credit earned on this trip would help them graduate. On this second trip, we noticed increased sharing during Circle, full participation in activities, independent high-order questioning, and an increased interest in social justice. The complex journal entries and videotapes documenting why this experience made our students more excited to learn moved us deeply. Five of those students now attend post-secondary programs, two dropped out of school, one received a High School Equivalency Diploma or HSED, and the others graduated from high school and are now working.

The third year, 2006, we focused on Western Expansion from a human rights perspective. We included more poetry and continued to deliver science lessons on geology, the environment and camping skills. During this trip, ten students worked extremely hard on assignments, taught their own mini-lessons, and learned to cooperate effectively. In addition, our restorative justice Circles were even more powerful. Students spoke openly and honestly about why this style of school appealed to them and frankly said that their engagement levels changed as a result. They also spoke of their awe of what we had seen in nature, and their sadness at the injustice that they saw presented through our Westward Expansion history lessons. But most often, without our prompting, students spoke of their connections to each other. Out of these students, one graduated on the trip, six graduated during the next two years of school, and three pursued their High School Equivalency Diplomas.

On each trip, these core pieces were part of our process:

- Experiential Learning
- Restorative Justice Circles
- Social Justice Curriculum
- Human Rights Education
- Camping Skills
- Environmental Education

The first foundation of this program is experiential education and hands-on learning. In experiential learning theory, ideas grow and change through experience (Kolb, 1984). Kraft and Sakofs (1988) describe experiential education as a process that actively engages students and allows students to experience new knowledge first hand. In experiential education, the reflection or debriefing process holds the key to transforming the skills, attitudes and theories held by students (Joplin, 1995). Our students' responses to hands-on learning, travel, and observing the historical sites directly will be presented in detail in Chapter Two.

Part of hands-on learning involves taking healthy risks and communicating with team members; thus, establishing a safe, trusting climate is essential, especially when working with students who have disengaged from traditional schooling. Because of this, the second foundation of our program is restorative justice Talking Circles. (Please note that the term "Circle" will be capitalized throughout the book as it is in most restorative justice literature.)

In an education system that often silences youth who are marginalized (Deschenes, Tyack, & Cuban, 2001), each year we form a caring community in which student voices are heard. Because our trips last twenty-four hours a day for over two weeks at a time, we have broken through the barriers built by structured bells and overwhelmingly large classes. Our "classroom time" starts at the crack of dawn with a morning meditation and lasts until midnight with final Circle. Although our itinerary is well planned, our moments of connection occur when we prepare food and share in meals together, when we all see an amazing view of nature and reflect on how it impacted us personally, when we play games during long stretches of driving and during many other times. This abundance of opportunity for connection is not present throughout a traditional school day. And yet, it needs to be. According to McNeely, Nonnemaker & Blum (2002):

> When adolescents feel cared for by people at their school and feel like a part of their school, they are less likely to use substances, engage in violence, or initiate sexual activity at an early age. Students who feel connected to school in this way also report higher levels of emotional well-being. (p. 138)

This is highly important when engaging learners who have become disillusioned by the educational system, as our students had been.

Angel Salathe, Randy Bauer, and I believe that connecting to one another and providing time to answer the big questions in life is as important as the science, social studies and English curriculum. We agree with Noddings (1995) who states:

> Some educators today—and I include myself among them—would like to see a complete reorganization of the school curriculum. We would like to give a central place to the questions and issues that lie at the core of human existence. (p. 675)

Our Circle process is that central place. It is during Circle that I feel true caring for others begins to develop. Noddings (1992) states that positive developments in adolescents are linked to the caring relationships within their lives, including schools. Yet in 2004, during the start of our program, Minnesota high school students reported in the 2004 Minnesota Survey that they didn't feel strongly cared about by teachers and other adults at school. Feelings of care were higher in sixth grade, with 28% of males and 30% of females reporting that they felt teachers and other adults cared about them "very much". However, the number drops significantly to 10% of ninth grade males and 9% of ninth grade females reporting feeling that teachers and adults cared about them "very much". That trend continues in twelfth grade with 10% of males and 11% of females feeling cared about "very much". (MN Department of Education, 2004, p. 13). Noddings (1992) says, "The current structures of schooling work against care, and at the same time, the need for care may be greater than ever" (p. 20). In a system focused on standardized tests, results and common assessments, when do we have time to care for our students, especially at the secondary level? When do students have time to reflect and honestly be listened to? Our program is the way that we broke down the current school structure in order to connect with our students. And it worked better than we could ever imagine. Further investigation of connectedness theory, restorative justice Talking Circles, and the results that Circle had on our youth will be discussed in Chapter Three.

Circle also connected students to concepts such as responsibility, care for each other, and social justice. For example, each year, we would spend one full day engaged in community service projects, such as working on fire prevention at a South Dakota camp for people with disabilities, rebuilding campsites and clearing litter at a horse camp in the Wyoming hills, and clearing litter and debris at campsites close to streams. We found that restorative justice Circles planted seeds about social justice, but could not stand alone in restoring justice, so we built a curriculum that cycled through human rights knowledge, provided time for reflection through Circle, presented students with planned opportunities to serve the environment and communities, and then returned to Circle each evening to reflect on their own social justice actions and responses. Thus, Circle was not held in isolation. As teachers, we believe strongly that providing opportunities for students to actively restore justice to people and land is paramount.

Another important factor of this program is that restorative justice Circles are combined with careful social justice curriculum. The curriculum uses critical reading and discussion to facilitate positions on human rights issues. Students learn of the human rights violations against Native Americans by visiting the Wounded Knee Museum and the Crazy Horse Memorial. They learn about the right to clean air and land, and begin actively caring for the wildlife areas that we visit. They study the diverse opinions of ranchers and scientists regarding the wolf population in Wyoming, and come to their own decisions on which side is "just." In addition, students study the history and meanings of Bears' Lodge, its renaming into Devil's Tower, and the opposing views held by climbers versus the people who believe that the site is a sacred monument. Again, students use their knowledge of human rights to create opinions of what is "just."

In addition to developing critical thinking around social justice issues, our program provides evidence that human rights curriculum, in partnership with environmental education, can facilitate changes within students—they can move from being disengaged from society (in some cases being juvenile delinquents in our court system) to being young social justice advocates. As our program developed, we focused more and more on human rights, agreeing with the theory that human rights education can promote peacemaking (Reardon, 1997). Because many of our students experience violence and oppression firsthand, glossing over ideas of "peace" and "justice" would have proven ineffective. Instead, we dig deeply into our own experiences and facilitate discussions on social activism. We model our practice around the belief that multicultural education is best served when it moves into the realm of social justice (Sleeter, 1996). And our students actively respond to this. Nieto (1992) writes that multicultural education was developed as a response to inequality in education based on racism, language discrimination, and ethnocentrism. Because our alternative students experienced these inequalities in both educational and judicial systems, they responded passionately to both human rights and social justice education. We will explore the curriculum and student responses to it in Chapter Four.

Along with research regarding the foundations that make up the program, this study details the changes that students documented— changes about beliefs, ideas, and practices. Thus, this study focuses on transformative learning theory in response to the use of outdoor education, hands-on learning, restorative justice Talking Circles, multicultural education, and human rights education.

In 1978, Jack Mezirow developed transformative learning theory during a study sponsored by the U.S. Department of Education that was investigating the large number of women returning to education in the United States (Mezirow, 1978). Results of the initial study showed that ten phases of learning were involved in the transformative process:

1. A disorienting dilemma
2. Self-examination
3. A critical assessment of assumptions
4. Recognition of a connection between one's discontent and the process of transformation
5. Exploration of options for new roles, relationships, and action
6. Planning a course of action
7. Acquiring knowledge and skills for implementing one's plan

8. Provisional trying of new roles
9. Building competence and self-confidence in new roles and relationships
10. A reintegration into one's life on the basis of conditions dictated by one's new perspective

(Mezirow, 1991, pp. 168–169/2009, p. 19)

According to Mezirow (1991) the transformational learning process is a shift in perspectives (p. 14). He describes the perspective transformation as:

> ...the process of becoming critically aware of how and why our assumptions have come to constrain the way we perceive, understand, and feel about our world; changing these structures of habitual expectation to make possible a more inclusive, discriminating, and integrating perspective; and finally, making choices or otherwise acting upon these new understandings. (Mezirow, 1991, p. 167)

Taylor writes that, "Fostering transformative learning is seen as teaching for change" (Taylor, 2009, p. 3). The program that we envisioned and created was admittedly built around the hope for change. Our goals as teachers were to re-engage our students, to create a safe climate, and to change student perspectives on learning (move them from disengagement to excitement about the learning process). Each student who applied to participate in the trip began the trip with goals such as earning credit and traveling. The changes that occurred were much deeper than we ever expected—both our goals, as well as our students' goals, paled in comparison to actual results. Unlearned in transformative learning theory, our practice was formed based on our knowledge at the time. Using intuition, past successes, personal experiences and big hearts, we crafted a program that promoted change. Unbeknownst to us at the time, our program fostered transformative learning. Taylor writes that the following core elements foster transformative educational experiences:

1. Individual experience
2. Critical reflection

3. Dialogue
4. Holistic orientation
5. Awareness of context
6. Authentic practice (Taylor, 2009, p. 4)

Individual experience consists of what each learner brings to the classroom (Taylor, 2009, p. 5). Our students brought immense experiences to our classroom and shared some of those experiences with us during the program. For example, one of our young students was pregnant and shared her fears about finding a place to stay and how she would raise her child. Another student had recently been arrested and spoke to us about serving time at a juvenile detention facility. One young woman shared her experiences with an addiction to methamphetamine. Others shared rich traditions about their beliefs, culture, and home lives. It is important here to note that transformative learning theory is an adult learning theory. Taylor (2000) writes:

> Only in adulthood are meaning structures clearly formed and developed and the revision of established meaning perspectives takes place. However, there has been little research to support this claim, such that transformative learning has not been explored in relationship to learning and the age of participants. (p. 288)

The age range in current documented studies is seventeen to seventy (Taylor, 2000). Most of our students were seventeen to nineteen years old, but we did have sixteen-year-old participants. However, our students were not "traditional" students. Their life experiences had forced some of them into early adulthood. Getting kicked out of the house, drug-addicted parents/guardians, personal addiction, pregnancy/parenting, and the foster care system had forced some of our participants into adult roles early on. Even the students who were still under the care of loving adults had experienced betrayals in their lives—betrayals by the education system (many were "pushed out" of mainstream classrooms) or betrayals by peers that made them "grow up fast." I would argue that our alternative students, though young, were prepared for transformative learning and that they should be part of communities that allow them to discuss and explore a wide range of topics. Belenky and Stanton (2000) agree and write that discourse communities, such as those fostering transformative learning, can include the immature and the marginalized (p. 74). Our students have been described as both. Though living under labels such as "at-risk," "marginalized," and "academically deficient" our students were prepared for change and volunteered for this program. Researchers don't rule out transformative learning in adolescents, it just isn't well studied or documented. Indeed according to Taylor (2000) transformative learning might "inform meaning-making during childhood or adolescence, particularly understanding the impact and the processing of significant trauma" (p. 289). As Hannah's opening quote stated, many students began processing traumas during the course of our program. For example, one student had been badly beaten and hospitalized prior to the trip and was able to process some of that experience through dialogue and rituals such as Circle. Age is a factor that needs to be studied in more detail regarding transformative learning, however, it is important to note that our students brought rich histories and life experiences into the classroom, that many had been pushed into adult roles at a young age, and that though "labeled" negatively by peers and school systems, our students were willing to take a risk and try something new.

Critical reflection and dialogue occurred during our program both informally while traveling and formally through restorative justice Talking Circles. Critical reflection refers to "questioning the integrity of deeply held assumptions and beliefs based on prior experiences" (Taylor, 2009, p. 7). Critical reflection was fostered through journal writing and exposure to new information about historical events such as Wounded Knee. Dialogue fosters transformation because it provides a safe place for learners to hear other opinions, gather details, share their assumptions, and voice new ideas (Mezirow, 2000). Our restorative justice Talking Circles built the trust that enabled the sharing of feelings to occur. These aspects will be discussed in chapters two and three.

The fourth core element that fosters transformative learning experiences, holistic orientation, concerns the practice of teaching. Are instructors engaging with multiple ways of knowing? Holistic orientation encourages both the affective and relational ways of knowing (Taylor, 2009). Affective knowing is described as the development of feelings and emotions in the reflective process (Taylor, 2009, p. 10). Emotions were definitely a part of our learning process. Both students and teachers shared a variety of emotions. Dirkx argues, "Helping learners understand and make sense of these emotion-laden experiences within the context of the curriculum represents one of the most important and most challenging tasks for adult educators" (1998, p. 9). Students' emotional reactions during the program were often deep and painful. I recall one student whose tears slid down her face for hours during a drive. When asked how she was doing, she responded, "I'm just working through so much right now. Out here with you all I can do that." Another student covered his head and cried and said, "How can you do this?" "What?" I asked. "Care about people like this? Love so much." I went on to explain that I just had to. That I felt more joy out of life when I loved than when I hid from love. In the case of this student, he was questioning his ideas about trust. Taylor states that emotions "often act as a trigger for the reflective process, prompting the learner to question deeply held assumptions" (Taylor 2009, p. 11). For these students, the emotions that they were feeling were raw. As a result, we felt it too. In most traditional classrooms, these conversations would never occur. Students would be told to leave their emotions at the classroom door. By nurturing the emotions, change could occur. Another aspect of holistic orientation involves including opportunities to experience presentational ways of knowing (Taylor, 2009, p. 11). We included music, physical activities such as paddling a river, quiet meditation time, poetry, myth, legend, and storytelling as forms of presentational ways of knowing. These expressive and physical arts, many that were new to students, also created seeds of new awareness. Documentation into these expressive arts and their impacts on transformative learning is now occurring. For example, Nelson (2009) documents that storytelling promotes transformational learning and resiliency in youth.

Awareness of context is the fifth core element that fosters transformative learning. Taylor writes that awareness of context is, "developing a deeper appreciation and understanding of the personal and socio-cultural factors that play an influencing role in the process of transformative learning" (Taylor, 2009, p. 11). This awareness of context was evident in two ways. The first is that students reported that they felt safer and more comfortable learning away from their own neighborhoods. They began speaking about friends, habits, and risk factors at home that stood in the way of their goals. We began processing ways to address that, yet this awareness of context provided a dilemma for us as teachers: how do we help our students to transition home? What can we do to encourage further transformation in their daily lives away from this experience? The second awareness of context involved cultural identity and race. Skin color and cultural practice impacted student understanding when it came to learning about the injustices done to Native Americans. Chapter Four records the depth of student experiences and our awareness of context when presenting our curriculum.

The final element is fostering authentic practice, including authentic relationships with students (Taylor, 2009). Building authentic relationships was very important to us as teachers. The three program leaders all shared the philosophy that relationship building was the primary objective in our educational practice. More on the importance of relationship building and our students' thoughts about relationships are presented in Chapter Three.

As an educator, my experiences with these twenty-nine students have been the best of my career. I have seen students transformed and believe that a combined program using hands-on learning, human rights education, multicultural education, social justice curriculum, and the use of Circles is the primary reason that students were able to share openly and honestly about their experiences, re-engage with an educational system that had failed them, and become interested in community again. Using a variety of research methods including examining student and teacher journals, conducting systematic observations of student behavior and interactions, and analyzing in-depth interviews with students and teaching staff, this book shows that these deeply disengaged students became active participants in their learning, developed closer bonds with each other and their teachers, and experienced transformations. It is their words that provide insight into why youth initially disengage with school, what types of learning that they prefer, and what they need in order to learn to trust again. If we want to re-engage our marginalized youth, we must listen carefully to their words.

I begin by taking a deeper look at one closing Circle held during June of 2006.

Westward Bound Expedition Closing Circle, June 2006

Campfire and Circle was a time that all of us looked forward to. The fire would blaze from Minneapolis through South Dakota and Wyoming. Sometimes small, sometimes large, the light would cast a glow that instilled an aura of trust. On this night, in June of 2006, tornado wall clouds, severe thunderstorm warnings, and four nights of straight rain drove three teachers and ten students to a motel in Wall, South Dakota. It was our last night together and a mixture of emotions was present. Would we still be able to come together in trust without the physical fire?

We all crowded into a hotel suite excited by the warmth of dry clothes and down quilts. I hopped from one of the beds and grabbed my orange sweatshirt from my pack. I gently placed it over the lamp and a subtle orange glow filtered through the room. "Well, this is our campfire tonight!" I said and then prepared to lead our final Circle.

We opened each nightly Circle with a ritual or devotion. Sometimes it was storytelling, sometimes quotes or readings. Tonight's ritual would serve as closure. We called it, "Leaving it in the Mountains." Stemming from my old summer camp counseling experiences, where one writes down issues or problems and burns it in the fire, we modified the activity and used the metaphor of leaving burdens in the Bighorn Mountains. Without a fire, we relied on students' trust of us…that his/her writing would remain confidential and would be burned in the fire by Mr. Bauer, our science teacher, upon our return home. Our students, labeled "at-risk" by the educational system, had faced many troubles in their short lives. And so they wrote and wrote. Some cried. Each folded their burdens into a tight fold of paper and set it beneath our lamp.

After this process, I began the second part of the evening's Circle by preparing to read a poem. We videotaped part of this campfire, with student permission, so my words, and theirs, are exactly as they were spoken.

I began:

> Final campfire on these trips is always something that is filled with mixed emotions because there's a complete feeling of happiness that you'll soon be home, in your bed, and yet you're feeling this mix of the unspoken, "Wow, next week, I'm not going to be with these people. I'm not going to see what I saw. And the chance of me seeing these things again in the next year are not very much." And so, you'll be feeling some mixed emotions with it. So, the poem today...this one is all about the connections that you've made to each other and that we've made with you. I was sitting and thinking when I was crying at McDonald's because I was so tired...that I also get really sad when the trips end because we really learn to love each of you. All of your idio- syncrasies, your helpfulness, your leadership, your intelligence, your ques- tioning skills, even at times when we can't answer those questions because we are concentrating on other things. We love you for those things and...this is all about us, right now. It's no longer about Devil's Tower or the Medicine Wheel. It's about us. And so, this final campfire is about that. This poem, called "Making Contact" is about that.

I read the poem, written by Virginia Satir (2003), aloud and asked for a student voice to read it aloud a second time. Following the pat- tern of the rest of the week, we then opened the silence up to anyone who wanted to share a line that stood out, or a thought that resonated with them.

Jackie responded without hesitation:

> I really relate to this poem, because, um. Terry, I've known him since he was younger and we didn't really like each other because we were totally differ- ent. And this trip, I thought, 'Is he going to be mean to me?' but we actually found out that we get along really pretty well. And I don't know, just with everybody. I made a connection with Hannah too. Just everyone.

About thirty seconds followed and Mr. Bauer began speaking:

I think an important line is the one talks about being understood. I think every human being, remember that we are social creatures, are not alone in this world and we need to be understood. When we aren't understood, there's a tremendous feeling of alienation and loneliness. However, the only way to be understood is to expose yourself. And it is a risk. And it takes courage. But there can be great reward for doing it. Remember to take that risk. Everyone is afraid of not being understood, and that's pretty painful, and that's a possibility. But you also have that other possibility which is that tremendous reward that you are understood by someone else. And that's a wonderful feeling.

Next, Suzy explored her thoughts:

The part that stuck out to me was the part about being seen. I felt that before the trip I wasn't a part of any group. And I feel that I now have a bigger connection with everybody. And, um, it was really nice to like, even when the teacher's asked me about my Dad, I was grateful that somebody actually understood the predicament that I'm in, and that my family is in. I've never really had the opportunity to talk about that and have people understand what I'm going through. I actually felt one with the group and that is really nice." (Suzy's father is wheelchair dependent. Suzy had a great experience when we did our community service project at a camp called "Meeting the Need" a camp in South Dakota geared towards making the Black Hills experience available to people with disabilities.)

"At some point in our life," began Jordan, "in everybody's life. They feel like they're a total outcast. And this is their goal—to be noticed by somebody."

Shelia, a student working through tremendous challenges, continued the dialogue:

For me, this is kind of like, I want to get back to that place where I can have that gift from people. Like, I'm sure you guys have all heard gossip, um, I've been dealing with some issues…oh, sad. I'm crying. Hold on. I need a second (Shelia allows the tears to run down her cheek, raising her hood for security)….For me, it's really, um, difficult to get to that place where I can be with people and be comfortable. Where I can give of myself. I feel like I haven't done that for you guys. I don't know if it matters to you, but…yeah, I would just like to get to that place again.

After another half hour of sharing, we closed our discussion of the poem and experienced the final phase of our Circle. Using a talking piece, each student shared his or her final thoughts about the two weeks we spent together. To honor the Circle, these moments were not recorded. They were special moments filled with laughter and more tears. Having no real campfire didn't matter. Trust had been formed early on and had stayed with this group. Our students had learned curriculum, camping skills and nature appreciation, but even greater than that knowledge, our disengaged students had transformed and learned to make contact with one another. Even if it wasn't the full contact that some desired, they had begun the process of reconnecting. This is just one of many transformations that will be discussed in this book.

CHAPTER TWO

Heading West: Hands-on Learning and Outdoor Education Increases Student Motivation

Over the course of the three separate Westward Bound summer school courses, hands-on learning and living within a natural setting were key elements of our program. In this chapter, I will provide a brief history and rationale for the inclusion of these elements. Using qualitative research methods, such as in-depth interviews during and after the course, as well as journal evidence, this study explores the following questions:

- What impact did hands-on learning and an outdoor experience have on our students?
- Did hands-on learning impact student motivation?
- Did either component foster transformative learning?

We begin by looking at the rationale, research, and experiences that guided our decision to include hands-on learning and experiences in nature as essential components of our program.

When Angel Salathe and I began planning our first trip, we wanted to focus on providing unique learning experiences for our students outside the traditional four walls of our classrooms. We agreed with current researchers who state that integrating authentic learning that is hands-on and minds-on makes learning more interesting (Smolleck, 2008). In regards to the "hands-on learning" aspects of our program, Angel, Randy, and I were influenced by theories of progressive education, outdoor education, and environmental education.

Learning by experience is often tied to the work of John Dewey and his theory of progressive education (Smith, Roland, Havens, and Hoyt, 1992). Kneller (1971) developed a list of lessons from Dewey's progressivism. The following lessons were present in the building of our program:

1. Education should be about life itself, not a preparation for living
2. Learning should be directly related to student interests
3. The school should encourage cooperation rather than competition (Kneller, 1971)

When considering that our student population was disengaged with schooling, and that many of our students had never worked together before, we designed our program around the ideas that education should be about life itself, and that cooperation is integral to success. We purposefully integrated a travel program that incorporated lessons on history, science, and writing with the day-to-day aspects of living. Students cooperated in tasks such as planning, purchasing, and preparing meals. We also developed clear rules that encouraged communication, such as requiring that students leave their iPods and cell phones at home. This enabled students and teachers to carry on discussions during the long drives. Sometimes the discussions were planned by the teacher and related to curriculum, and sometimes the discussions were spontaneous and based on the needs and interests of the students. Even these moments of driving, enabled students to learn more about each other and share in an experience together.

In addition, we utilized cooperative learning strategies developed by Spencer Kagan, a model of cooperative learning adopted by our district, to promote engaging experiences. Cooperative learning is a teaching arrangement that refers to small, heterogeneous groups of students working together to achieve a common goal (Kagan, 1994). Spencer Kagan's model includes the following four elements:

1. Positive Interdependence—occurs when gains of individuals or teams are positively correlated
2. Individual Accountability—occurs when all students in a group are held accountable for doing a share of the work and for mastery of the material to be learned

3. Equal Participation—occurs when each member of the group is afforded equal shares of responsibility and input
4. Simultaneous Interaction—occurs when class time is designed to allow many student interactions during the period (Kagan, 1994)

One example of the way that we included Kagan (1994) structures is during our pre-trip courses. The courses varied from four-weeks of one class period per day to five consecutive eight-hour days. (These differences were based on staffing or funding at the time per administrative requests.) When Angel, Randy, and I switched to five full days of classroom instruction, we knew that it could be overwhelming for students, so we focused on a great deal of simultaneous interaction. The first day, we did an activity called Corners (Kagan, 1994) so that students could begin to connect with each other. In Corners (Kagan, 1994), we pointed to different corners in the room based on the following statements: "I'm a camping pro"; "I'm a city person through and through"; "I like the outdoors, but haven't camped"; "I dislike the outdoors". Students then discussed their experiences in small groups. I then asked for a volunteer to share a whole-group summary. This activity not only allowed students to connect, but it allowed us to hear about the experiences students have had and to learn more about his/her background with the outdoors. We also used Jigsaw (Kagan, 1994), a structure that encourages interdependence. Each student on a team of four was given the name of an explorer to study. Using the books provided and the Internet, the student became an "expert" on their topic. They then returned to their group, shared the information and created a timeline about the explorers. We saw that all the structures encouraged communication, team-building, and content mastery. All students, including those with disabilities, passed each content mastery test that we administered. The use of cooperative learning structures also kept the day interesting for the students and kept lectures and direct-instruction down to less than one hour per day.

Many researchers agree that using cooperative learning in the classroom can benefit all students, whether the student is gifted, low achieving, or a student with special needs (Augustine, Gruber, and Hanson, 1989/ 1990). This was significant in our planning, as our students ranged in academic levels from those with learning disabilities to those scoring extremely high on standardized tests. Cooperative learning has also been shown to enhance social interactions, which is a key component in the success of students labeled "at-risk" (Slavin, Karweit, and Madden, 1989). This aspect of Dewey's philosophy, administered by instructors who all received training in Kagan Cooperative Learning Structures and had great buy-in to the program, increased our student's success in the classroom as evidenced through high levels of engagement, increased motivation to complete assigned tasks, passing exam scores, and an overall environment of excitement and full-participation. Other studies conducted by Kagan-trained teachers have also found increased achievement in student learning (Dotson, 2001; Heusman and Moenich, 2003).

Our program also had philosophical roots tied to Kurt Hahn (Flavin, 1996; Hahn, 1957). Hahn, best known for founding Outward Bound, believed that a group could be used to mirror a mini-community resulting in a shared experience that could help people learn to work together (Itin, 1999). Another study conducted in the field of experiential education and adventure programs found that adolescents showed significant changes regarding social acceptance (Garst, Scheider & Baker, 2001). Through activities such as white-water rafting, community service, and camp preparation, we saw students who couldn't cooperate effectively at the beginning of the trip begin to work together. For example, students who wouldn't speak to each other at school were encouraging each other to participate in new things, such as white-water rafting.

In regard to outdoor education, we agree with Berman and Davis-Berman (1995) who state that traditional education programs can inhibit the emotional growth and education of some individuals and that outdoor programs offer a new way for staff and students to approach each other through shared activities. Berman and Davis-Berman state, "Outdoor programs also place troubled youth in unique settings where they are often unsure of themselves. Moving

out of the usual environment sometimes serves to reduce defensive-
ness and change relationships with adult leaders" (1995, ¶ 8). We also
hypothesized that removing troubled urban youth from their home
environments, teaching them new skills, such as camping, and providing them with the opportunity to learn in beautiful outdoor places
would re-engage them in the education process; thus, we began linking our curriculum with our appreciation of the outdoors. We
planned our drive through Minnesota, South Dakota, North Dakota,
and Wyoming based on Westward Expansion history. As we looked
at maps, selected campsites, and planned our trip, we were constantly
aware of the outdoor experiences that were possible.

Outdoor education dates back to Lloyd B. Sharp's work in the
1930s. He believed that subjects that could be taught in the outdoors
should be taught in the outdoors (Smith, Roland, Havens, and Hoyt,
1992). Throughout the 1970s, the emphasis on outdoor education as
an extension of standard curriculum continued to grow (Smith, Roland, Havens, and Hoyt, 1992). Randy had the privilege of learning in
the outdoors through experiences in the Boy Scouts and community
organizations. Angel and I had the experience of growing up on or
near farms where we learned through outdoor experiences every day.
In addition, my father, a high school biology teacher, took his students on camping and field trips to the North Dakota Badlands. As a
student who participated in these experiences, I saw firsthand how
science curriculum, such as geology, could become interesting to all
students when studied in an outdoor setting. Indeed researchers pro-
pose that natural settings stimulate children's development in unique
ways by demanding visualization, incorporating the full use of the
senses, promoting imagination through play, and encouraging physical movement (Louv, 2005; Moore, 1997). Children in natural settings
also demonstrate growth in physical, social and emotional development as well (Gostev and Weis, 2007; Moore, 1997). The social and
emotional development of our youth was on our minds as we
planned our trips, as many of our students were struggling with social and emotional issues such as drug abuse, alienation from family,
and low achievement in school or jobs. Significantly, evidence also

suggests that participants in outdoor education programs experience additional growth on returning to their home environments (Neil and Richards, 1998). Additional research shows that adventure education, such as the white-water rafting experience that we included in our program, decreases student perceptions of alienation (Cross, 2002). This research guided our belief that an immersive experience in nature be an essential piece of the program.

The final component of the hands-on learning part of Westward Bound was our belief in the power of environmental education. A working definition of environmental education was developed at an IUCN/UNESCO conference entitled, "International Working Meeting on Environmental Education in the School Curriculum" held in 1970. It states:

> Environmental education is the process of recognizing values and clarifying concepts in order to develop skills and attitudes necessary to understand and appreciate the inter-relatedness among man, his culture, and his bio-physical surroundings. Environmental education also entails practice in decision-making and self-formulation of a code of behavior about issues concerning environmental quality. (Palmer, 1998)

Environmental education is interdisciplinary, uses the environment to stimulate realistic activities and to promote investigation, and focuses on improving and conserving the environment (Palmer, 1998). We found that environmental education was indeed interdisciplinary, as we incorporated lessons of science, literature, mathematics, and social studies with ease (Smolleck, 2008). When planning our curriculum, we worked together to develop team teaching in which Randy, Angel and I all studied the topics that students would explore. Though one of us was the "expert" in each field, we each could provide general information about the history of the West, the geology of the Badlands, and different styles of writing. Throughout the program, environmental education was a key theme. In addition to conducting our teaching outdoors, we provided students with lessons on wilderness etiquette, we explored the results of human interactions with the natural environment, and we taught historical facts about the decimation of the bison herd. Students also completed an environmental education service project, in which a wilderness area received physical attention and advocacy.

Along with these philosophical foundations, we focused on promoting student interest and motivation. From studies we know that lack of motivation and interest is one reason why students drop out of school (Bridgeland, Dilulio, and Morison, 2006). In a survey conducted with ten students prior to participating in our 2006 program, nine out of ten students answered the statement, "I am often bored in school" with Strongly Agree. Nine out of ten students wrote that their interest in school curriculum and books used in their classes was "very low." Ainley (2006) describes interest in the following way:

> In summary interest as the immediate reaction to a new learning task is an affective state that involves feelings of arousal, alertness, attention and concentration and is a key variable in the motivation of learning. Interest as general orientation, or individual interest, is also a key factor contributing to on-task feelings of activation and interest and engagement in learning. (p. 399)

Research also states that interest is the most important form of intrinsic motivation (Artelt, 2005). In order to build on student individual interests, our alternative school already provided programs, such as independent study opportunities and some project-based learning; however, the students selected to participate in our program felt that even these alternative opportunities often lacked interest for them. In an interview one student said, "Even if the topic that I chose (for independent study) was interesting, I didn't feel motivated to do the work."

Other students shared this disconnect between interest and motivation as well. In the survey taken before starting the 2006 Westward Bound program, nine out of ten students answered, "I feel motivated in school" with Strongly Disagree. This is not surprising, as research by Oliver (1995) shows that the following factors are likely to decrease motivation: pregnancy (one of our students was pregnant at the time of the trip, two students were already fathers); being behind in grade-level and exhibiting poor academics (all of our students were behind at least one-year in school); dislike of school (nearly all of our students had histories of truancy); emotional problems or undiagnosed disabilities (both were present in the histories of 20 out of the 29 students participating in the Westward Bound program) and language difficulties (four of our students entered the public school system as English Language Learners). This research, and the connection that it had to our students, is concerning, as motivation has an impact on student engagement and academic achievement, especially in regard to literacy (Gambrell, 2001). Motivation has been defined as the energy and desire that is innate within all individuals (McDevitt and Ormrod, 2004). When planning the Westward Bound program, we incorporated elements that promoted motivation, such as creating a "web of social relationships that support learning" (Committee on Increasing, 2003). The web began with inviting parents/guardians to attend a meeting prior to the course. This meeting detailed the program and invited parents/guardians to encourage their student as they prepared for the trip. The meeting also provided the opportunity to complete forms, discuss any medical concerns, dietary needs, and educational needs. The next part of the web was building student-teacher relationships.

Since student-teacher relationships influence motivation, we were committed to fostering positive interactions, remaining enthusiastic, and providing positive feedback (Rugutt and Chemosit, 2009). We avoided teacher behaviors linked to low motivation such as lack of enthusiasm for what we were teaching and providing little choice for our students (Brewster and Fager, 2000). Most of the students already knew at least two teachers prior to the trip, but we knew that a deeper relationship would encourage motivation and growth. Strong student-teacher relationships would have a positive impact on all of our students; however, based on the trends at our alternative school, our Native American and Hmong students were particularly at risk of dropping out. Powers (2005) writes:

> Strong relationships between students and teachers promote a sense of belonging, freedom to take academic risks, and investment in academic learning (i.e., academic motivation), and may help American Indian students negotiate cultural discontinuities between school and home. (¶ 15)

Thus, the first days of our in-school sessions contained a great deal of time for relationship building through games and story telling. The final component in the web was promoting positive student-student relationships. We used restorative justice Talking Circles as a way to connect students to each other. More details on this strategy will follow in Chapter Three.

Another element that promotes motivation is active participation and "hands-on learning" (Committee on Increasing, 2003). According to Guthrie, "Teachers can increase student motivation through creative engagement by using stimulating tasks. Tasks that stimulate students to think in new ways, such as hands-on activities, have lasting effects on motivation and comprehension" (Guthrie, et al., 2006, p. 234). Hands-on learning refers to social structures that promote active participation and feelings of belonging (Box and Little, 2003). As stated by Jalongo, a better term for hands-on learning might be "minds-on," because "such learning goes beyond physical interaction with materials to build the learners' confidence and skill in advancing their understandings" (Jalongo, 2007, p. 398). As previously stated, when we began to build the Westward Bound curriculum, we knew that our summer school "in-class" days would be six to eight hours long. Thus, active learning through games, activities, and physical movement that related to the curriculum was very important. For example, after discussing the history of the gold rush, we developed a game of hide-and-seek tag, in which students had to find bags of gold and then get the gold to a location without being stopped and tagged by different students. Understanding that relevance also influences motivation, we also taught students practical things like how to put up their tents, some basics of orienteering, wilderness safety, and how to pack efficiently (Harada & Yoshina, 2004). Because students knew that all of those skills would be useful, motivation was high. All students actively participated in the activities, laughed, and built relationships during the time. In addition, students consistently scored 90% or above on quizzes. Plus, the upcoming trip itself, increased motivation. This was detailed in a description from my observational journal:

Guy began to close his eyes and admits that he's sleepy today. During Angel's presentation on the Great Plains, she said, "And you'll get to see that."
He became completely alert after that and stays alert through the next 15
minutes of the presentation until break.

This type of interest is called "situational interest." Situational interest is a spontaneous and short-lived interest based on the experience itself, but it has a strong effect on attitudes towards engagement
and learning (Jalongo, 2007). Researchers are beginning to make connections between situational interest and building motivation (Guthrie, et al., 2006, and Ainley, 2006). Ainley argues:

> From what we know it is clear that there are at least two main routes to trig-
> gering interest in learning, one builds on knowledge of situational interest,
> the other on knowledge of individual interest. Situational interest can be
> triggered through attention to the way learning is presented... Triggering
> interest activates a system that generates positive feelings, focuses attention
> on the object that has triggered interest, and in the absence of stronger com-
> peting motives will prompt cognitive activity. (pp. 404–405)

Recognizing Lumsden's (1999) assertions that students want and
need work that stimulates their curiosity and arouses their desire for
deep understanding, we briefly introduced each historical and natural site that we would be seeing while allowing students to develop
their own questions about each topic. We then encouraged them to
record those questions and then answer them during our days on the
road. In addition to developing questions, I noticed an increased motivation for students to read about the sights that we would be seeing
as well. Books and resources were piled around the classroom and we
often asked students to dive into a book and tell us what they learned.
Even during breaks, students would be flipping through the books on
the Old West and Native American culture. However, it was during
the trip that we saw the situational interest of experiences build into
students' general interests in history, science, and writing.

The research methodology selected was a qualitative research
approach because I believe that focusing on the key experiences felt
by participants both during and after the course are valuable (Patton,
2002). All students from the 2004 and 2006 trips were invited to par-

ticipate in interviews or to submit their journals for study. Eighteen students supplied journals or participated in interviews. During both the 2004 and 2006 trip, students were interviewed one-on-one during one of the evenings of the trip. Though usually tired after long days of driving, exploring, and preparing camp, students talked for fifteen to twenty minutes. With their permission, the interviews were taped for research purposes. During all three trips students wrote in journals multiple times per day. We taught students the difference between objective and subjective journaling and students were required to record objective observations about what they saw in nature each day. They were also encouraged to record subjective entries of their thoughts and feelings. Angel, Randy, and I kept our own journals and observational notes on student participation and motivation. After analyzing the interviews and journals, I found that students spoke of the following elements having an impact on the transformative learning that occurred: hands-on, spontaneous learning; the separation of students from their lives at home; the spiritual and emotional responses to nature; and the outdoor challenges. Students reported that these elements also had an impact on their motivation to learn.

Factors That Influenced Transformative Learning:
Hands-on Spontaneous Education

Mezirow defines transformation as "a movement through time of reformulating reified structures of meaning by reconstructing dominant narratives" (Mezirow 2000, p. 19). According to Mezirow, transformative learning is about "how we learn to negotiate and act on our own purposes, values, feelings, and meanings rather than those we have uncritically assimilated from others—to gain greater control over our lives as socially responsible, clear thinking decision makers" (Mezirow, 2000, p. 8). He goes on to state that people transform frames of reference by becoming self-reflective about their assumptions and aware of the contexts that influenced those assumptions (Mezirow, 2000). Disorienting dilemmas are described by Mezirow as one of the phases of meaning that transformation often includes (2000, p. 21). According to Clark (2008), "a disorienting dilemma is related to a sense of loss of balance or normalcy complicated by a problem that seemingly has an unsatisfactory solution" (p. 47). Disorienting dilemmas can be internal or external moments of personal crises (Mezirow, 1978). In the case of our students one disorienting dilemma for them had been "failing" out of the traditional high school setting. When asked about past education experiences, all 2006 students who were interviewed said that they had negative perceptions of school. Nine students spoke of feeling like a "failure" when they had to move to our alternative school. They held assumptions that any school experience must be met with a certain level of distrust and pessimism. In an interview Hannah said, "When I fell really behind in mainstream, I kind of just quit asking for help. It just all seemed kind of pointless." In some cases, students were carrying a belief that they had been pushed out of their traditional schools because they didn't fit the mold of a "good student." Clyde said, "They (school officials) basically just want you to fail so that they can get you out of there. They just don't believe that you need help and think you're just having an attitude problem." Clyde's response aligns with Smyth's (2010) research on connectedness and dropping out. Smyth writes:

> At a more personal level, power relations are played out on a daily basis in classrooms as young people contest authoritarian and autocratic relationships which they see as being out of kilter with contemporary life. This process of contestation and "speaking back" in the quest for a more democratic space, often leads to situations in which the burden of undemocratic school cultures is often borne by students. (p. 200)

Clyde said that whenever he "spoke out" because he felt that something was unfair he would receive detentions, which eventually led to truancy issues. In order to be open to the possibility of learning during Westward Bound, our students would have to reflect critically on their assumptions about school and we would have to supply a nurturing "democratic space" in which they could succeed.

O'Sullivan (2002) speaks of transformative learning in terms of homeostatic negative feedback and adaptive positive feedback. With homeostatic feedback, one is on track and has no need to make adjustments. Adaptive positive feedback, however, occurs when there is a mismatch between perception and code in which one needs to correct or alter their course. Adaptive positive feedback means that we can no longer, "interpret experience in terms of our old assumptions" (O'Sullivan, 2002, p. 3). The cognitive system then searches for new codes. Although O'Sullivan's idea is complex, aspects of it can be applied to our students. Prior to the trip many students spoke of having low motivation and a disinterest in school subjects. The "code" that many of our students worked under was an assumption that school would always be boring and that no one cared about their success. Suddenly, they were faced with a mismatch between perception and code—they were enjoying their educational experience. Guy said, "I really thought this trip would be boring and just like a school day. I suddenly realized that I was having a lot of fun, especially when we got to the Badlands. It all made me think differently about learning."

Others, such as Margaret, describe shifts in their perceptions of school and learning. Margaret's story documents an individual whose idea of learning shifted with her alternative education experiences, specifically within our program. I first met Margaret her ninth-grade-year when I taught at a traditional high school. Margaret would often sleep through classes, and spoke of problems with alcoholism and poverty in her family life. When Margaret moved to the alternative school she attended classes and was more alert, but she still was not motivated to complete homework outside of the school day. Recovering credits was very difficult because of her lack of motivation to attend night school or to turn in any independent study work (both were ways that students could recover credits in our district). I encouraged Margaret to attend our summer school program in order to recover some missing science and English credit. During the Westward Bound program, Margaret's responses to education were very different than what instructors had previously witnessed. Margaret was constantly reading, completing thoughtful journals, and participating in scientific inquiry and experiments. In addition, my observational journal recorded that Margaret asked staff complex, interesting questions. Margaret had this to say about learning during Westward Bound:

When I go on field trips like this, I learn more because you actually get to see stuff, instead of just reading about it. It keeps me interested. You don't get to just see pictures in the textbook, you get to see the stuff one on one and live. Like seeing it makes me more interested and makes me want to learn more, especially about social studies and science and stuff like doing experiments. It helps me learn better when I actually get to do experiments than just hearing about what it does and stuff because you actually get to do it.

Throughout the trip, Margaret was able to critically reflect on the types of learning experiences that helped her be successful. During campfire discussions and during one-on-one time with teachers, Margaret spoke of her shifts in ideas about learning. She was able to articulate why "seeing things" helped her understand scientific concepts such as river rates, geological formations, and migratory patterns. And the transformative power of this experience had a lasting impact on her. Her motivation levels increased during the school year following Westward Bound. As her Homeroom advisor, I witnessed Margaret advocating for her education by requesting classes that she knew held more hands-on learning opportunities. She also began turning in more Independent Study homework, especially homework that involved hands-on processes.

Hannah, a participant in our 2006 program, had this to say about the hands-on aspect of Westward Bound during a post-trip interview:

Hannah: The trip itself was amazing and I hold more information from this trip than any of the classes I'm taking now. When you learn by touching and feeling and experience, it really makes you realize what's around you, what else there is to comprehend.

Amy: In what way?

Hannah: Well, I look at everything in more detail now. I notice more things. I don't know—it's hard to explain. I just see more than I did before, so I'm able to learn more.

This observation, that there is more to comprehend than what is set before you, is significant. Hannah didn't enjoy traditional "banking" models of education, where the educational goal was to deposit information (Freire, 1970). But she thrived in the Westward Bound environment and in other alternative experiences offered at our school. Hannah's claim that she "held more information from this trip" is also significant. Mezirow describes learning as "the process of using a prior interpretation to construe a new or revised interpretation of the meaning of one's experience as a guide to future action" (Mezirow, 2000, p. 5). For Hannah, touching, feeling and experiencing history and science firsthand helped her develop an even greater awareness of what is around her now. It's almost as if Hannah is describing an awakening of her senses. Dirkx (1998) states that in transformative learning "learners work together with each other and with the educator to construct visions that are more meaningful and holistic, that lead them to deeper engagements with themselves and the world" (p. 10). In Hannah's case she was describing a holistic response to the program's hands-on aspect—it helped her begin to "see more" which now helps her to "learn more."

In an interview held during the 2004 trip, James also mentions that he learned better in a hands-on environment. He explains:

> Yeah, I learned better out here. For example, if you just learn in school and learn about Indians and the wars or famous leaders, you kind of learn about it and then you forget about it cuz you got other stuff you need to do. But this kind of thing, when you actually take a week and go to the places where battles were fought, and you go to museums and stuff—it's not just in the classroom. You get to see a lot more stuff. It helps you understand better, I thought. We'd learn about it in the classroom, and then we came out here. And so when we saw things, we knew what we were seeing. Whereas if you just came out here, you'd want to know who these people were. Or if you just went in the classroom, you wouldn't remember it.

Jackie, a member of the 2006 trip, also shared insights into the hands-on aspect of learning:

> I would love to go on another trip like that. You really do learn a lot. You do. When you see it, you learn way better than when you read a book, because reading a book you have to use your imagination and stuff and some people don't have that good of an imagination, they lose that. And some people can't picture a book. When you're out there and actually doing it, you remember like if you smell a certain smell it will bring you back to when you learned about a certain thing or if you hear a certain word it will

trigger something...When you're reading a book you don't remember. It is just words on a piece of paper.

Student motivation was also influenced by the fact that students were able to learn through spontaneous educational experiences. Jackie, a member of the 2006 trip, perceived that learning was "fun" because it was hands-on and spontaneous:

The trip overall was so much fun learning all the things...I remember when I was driving in Bauer's car, and everyone was sleeping in the back and we had a really bad storm—it was when we were coming back from Devil's Tower. We had like the worst luck ever—and we were looking at the clouds and they were so neat, but I was afraid we were gonna have a tornado, and I'm sitting there asking Bauer, "What do those clouds mean?" and "What kind of clouds are those?" I was just asking all kinds of questions and I was learning all kinds of weather information. And some things he didn't know and I'd get him stuck on a question. It was just always fun to be able to ask someone who knows all this science stuff. And when I was driving with Salathe and we started talking about how the hills had formed and that the plates had risen up and back then it was ice too and the thing that makes me remember those is that it was a memory of being able to see the land, and being with them, and learning about it. You actually get to see it in person. It's not like a picture you see—you see all these different shapes, you don't just see one shape from a picture. You see the whole land and it's just open and South Dakota is just beautiful all around. I want to go back there again soon.

Jackie's interview was held four months after her participation in the program and her excitement was still evident. She spoke of being able to ask questions based on her current experience. These spontaneous moments of learning occurred often on the trip. Angel recalls another moment of spontaneous learning:

On the way to the Grand Tetons, Wyoming, we stopped in the mountains to do a heart rate exercise. While doing that, two students said, "Hey Mr. Bauer... check this out!" They had spotted some tracks in the mud. Not sure what they were, they wanted Bauer's "expertise." However, Bauer didn't tell them... instead he had them get some info on tracks from his file as he pulled out his plaster cast materials and mixed up a batch. As we waited for it to dry, most of the students were looking around for other tracks. It inspired conversation about what type of animal might have left that track.

Elk? Deer? Horse? Free Range cow? What? It then motivated students to study the sheets Bauer had brought along and continue down the slope looking for more tracks. Once the mold was dried, cleaned, and studied, the answer was: ELK. We heard one student say, "See, I told you."

Angel recalled another moment:

I remember back to the time on the first trip when we all experienced, together, the rise of a midwestern thunderstorm rolling in across the plains at your parent's house in North Dakota. We could see it coming for miles. Then, you and Tommy walked out in the long prairie grass to watch the thunderstorm come in. The lightning flashed across the sky. The spiritual experience of it all. The buzz around the house as all of the other students waited while you and Tommy sat outside amazed by the power of such unquestioned phenomena. The other students were intrigued as well, but felt safer being in the house and watching from afar. What I remember went down something like this: Questions of all sorts blew out of their mouths like the strength of the NW wind... critical thinking at its best and a motivation, a thirst to WANT TO KNOW MORE. Questions like, "What causes lightning? How far away is the storm? Well, how do you know that?" Students were asking questions and others answered them. I recall the conversation about the number of seconds between lightning and thunder and the amount of miles away the storm is. I was dumbfounded that our city students would know the ways of the early pioneers in such a manner. Other questions like "Will there be a tornado?" and concerns shared such as, "I am really scared. What will we do if there is?" SURVIVAL on the plains. Ahh yes. Others reassuring the girl that the lowest point in the house, in it's SE corner would keep us safe. REALLY? REALLY? I did not have to answer any of the questions. They were facilitating their own learning experience. I merely sat back and observed what I was seeing and hearing, taking it all in as though I was the student who was the sponge! What more could a teacher want? You do not experience this type of learning within the confines of the classroom. That is the type of learning that is priceless.

According to Nohl (2009), "Spontaneity marks the boundaries of what is feasible in education" (¶ 3). As instructors, we tried to plan for some of these spontaneous moments and tried to push the boundaries of our curriculum. For example, Randy created curriculum boxes of extra information on over sixty possible science experiences from making casts of animal prints, information on animals that we might see, astronomy lessons, geology, and many other topics.

Angel and I packed books on Westward Expansion, Native American culture, and Old West stories and lore. We allowed our ideas about curriculum and learning to be flexible, yet we packed resources so that we could "jump-in" with information and mini-lessons when our experiences offered spontaneous opportunities. This ability to be both flexible, and intuitive, provided great teachable moments. In many cases, we were able to predict some of the questions regarding interests that our students had. When we couldn't answer a question it was exciting to see students motivated to ask park rangers, museum staff, or consult the books and resources that we had packed. Despite all that we had prepared, many of these spontaneous educational moments were unplanned and student directed. Their curiosity about events happening in the moment drove students to become engaged in problem solving, questioning, or journaling.

Nohl (2009) argues that spontaneous action plays a role in transformative learning. He states, "in the spontaneity of action, novelty finds its way into life, gains momentum, is respected by others and reflected by the actor" (¶ 2). Nohl found that his subjects participated in something new that they perceived as "different" and found fascinating, such as a engaging in a new art or technology. They then reflected on the experience and entered a phase of inquiry and learning. They then presented this new ability or art to others and continued exploring the spontaneous action (Nohl, ¶ 15–31). In some cases, our students went through a similar phase. For example, Jackie was a self-proclaimed "city girl," but spontaneous moments of engaging with the natural world caused her to reflect on her relationship with nature and to inquire about science and nature. She stated that when she returned home she "told anyone who would listen" about the trip. She then said that she wanted to return to South Dakota and Wyoming again and to have campfires by the river in Minnesota. It is not clear from the results of this study if spontaneous moments of learning as I have described led to spontaneous actions. Nor is it clear what role these moments had in transformative learning. I do believe that these spontaneous moments were factors that influenced students' reflections about learning and their role in it; however, more research needs to be conducted in this area.

Factors That Influenced Transformative Learning: Separation from "Normal" Life

In a study on outdoor adventure education and transformative learning D'Amato and Krasny (2009) found Outdoor Adventure Education alumni stated that experiencing a different lifestyle was a factor in their transformative process. They write:

> The process of leaving home, immersing in a different environment, and returning home, was a catalyst for personal growth. The isolation of participants from their usual relationships provided opportunities for trying out new behaviors....These factors may have contributed to transformative learning in that they represented a discrepant dilemma (Mezirow, 2000) in the participants' normal lives (p. 7–8).

James recognized that being away from "outside influences" helped him reflect:

> I think the field trip experiences are good because you don't really have the outside influences like you do at home that kind of make you lazy or make you not want to do it. This takes yourself away from your home. It's taking a whole week to do work instead of taking home homework and stuff and trying to do it when all your buddies are there. Schools should do more of this kind of stuff. For one, it brings people closer together, and two, it's a good educational experience.

James's observation that being away from home helped him stay engaged is important for youth labeled "at-risk." James, behind on credits, often spent time with friends after school rather than doing independent study. Prior to participating in the Westward Bound program, he openly admitted to using marijuana often. Because of the large population of drug users in our school, students needed to sign sobriety contracts to participate in the trip and were referred to counselors if they were open to seeking help. Though James was worried about staying sober, during the trip James said, "I'm so busy seeing new things and having fun that I haven't really thought about it much." Four other students who admitted to using drugs such as marijuana and cocaine prior to the trip reported similar results. These results in no way imply that all addicted adolescents need is an experiential education program; however, the student success during the program, and their motivation to become sober prior to the trip, cannot be overlooked. The trip did not lead to recovery for all the students, but one student said, "After the trip, I really started to think about being completely sober all the time. I started going to A.A. meetings." Though research is being developed on the impact of outdoor education and adventure education on adolescents facing substance abuse problems, more research is needed in that area of inquiry (Hill, 2005).

Being away from home was a disorienting dilemma for many students. Some students had a very difficult time not calling or texting friends or family. Others had a difficult time being away from city noises. Simple things like food and bathing were very different compared to students' normal lives. Measuring the impact that being away from home had on participants' transformative learning experiences is difficult to do. My interview questions did not directly address being away from home, but four students spoke of that in their interviews. Some research is being done in the area of study abroad programs and exchange programs (Warner and Kirby, 2010), but more research needs to be conducted in the area of travel as a factor in transformative learning.

Factors That Influenced Transformative Learning: Nature

D'Amato and Krasny's (2009) study on outdoor education and transformative learning found that all twenty-three participants interviewed reported that having access to pristine natural environments was personally significant (pp. 5–7). All of our students also brought up nature during their interviews. They reflected on specific memories or spoke of how their experiences in nature inspired new ways of thinking. As teachers, Randy, Angel, and I noticed transformations in the ways that students were expressing their learning. For example, moments in nature inspired high-level questioning and detailed writing, facilitated discussion and reflection, and sparked curiosity about science. In addition, moments in nature showed that our alternative students were resilient in the face of nature's obstacles.

In regard to resiliency, our 2006 trip members faced severe thunderstorms almost nightly. Faith, a 2006 participant, wrote in her journal:

> Last night was a very interesting night. Almost everybody's tent got water in it. Some of us slept in the van and it was very uncomfortable. But it was a funny night seeing everyone's tent get destroyed.

The way that students learned from these experiences and their attitudes towards the experiences inspired us as educators. Our students had never participated in a weeklong camping trip before. They could have very easily become angry, frustrated, or unmotivated because of these nightly storms and lack of sleep. However, they remained resilient and optimistic. Randy shared thoughts about this in his interview. He said:

> Last June after the violent thunderstorm the first night, I looked and I saw it and we were out in the open and I knew that we were gonna get pasted and we did. When I saw that the wind had blown half the tents down, I thought, this has done it…this will be the dagger in the heart of the field trip. Good god…there's nothing worse for a kid to wake up their first night camping and have their sleeping bag be soaking wet! So, you know, my tent, I don't care. I can withstand anything in that tent and I'm used to being wet, the tents leaking, I move over, I can figure stuff out. I know what to expect. But with the students, the kids, it's different. They don't know. Well, anyway, the tent is down and is collapsed, and I hear all this talking. I hear all this grumbling, and then I hear Tom chime up—"Hey, this is really cool. The sleeping bag floats." I could think of ten thousand other scenarios besides that that are negative, yet here's a kid—this is where students will completely fool you and they'll just say these things—that is the neatest comment because it meant that they were just taking this in stride. We had a crappy night, but they were able to find something cool about it. That is one moment that I remember really, really well.

This resiliency is something that we all admire about our alternative students. Though each student had faced huge challenges in his/her life, he/she continued to come to school. They continued to trust us during the trip, despite the challenges of nightly winds and rain. They problem-solved together, and we often overheard them working through ideas about drying gear, positioning their tents to protect against wind, and keeping their sleeping bags dry. They learned new camping skills after each night, and by the end of the trip, had tents fortified with duct tape. Their ability to laugh in the face of frustrating occurrences amazed us. Educators need to capitalize on these assets, rather than assuming that students labeled "at-risk" have deficits when it comes to new experiences. I've heard both administrators and teachers say things such as, "Well, these aren't the types of kids that you can take anywhere," or "At-risk kids can't handle things outside of their routine." These ideas leave little room for engaging students or motivating students to learn. Schools often lock students labeled "at-risk" into a formulized model of removing students from experiences, rather than offering new ones. It is true that some students have unique disabilities or risk behaviors that may interfere with some programs; however, the vast majority of students labeled "at-risk" will respond positively to new experiences as long as educators plan carefully, have trusting student-teacher relationships, and provide guidance and support should a negative experience occur. Our students were able to gracefully maneuver through the negative experiences and often turned them into positive memories that they laughed at. They were motivated to learn by all that Mother Nature provided, including the storms.

Students also responded with motivation to the beauty that they found in Nature. As their English teacher, I noticed an increase in descriptive language in student writing. These journal excerpts show that nature not only motivated and inspired students to learn, the experiences also brought out great detail in their writing, both scientific knowledge and imagery.

James wrote:

> In the foothills you can see the snow topped mountains. Scenery around here is gorgeous. Mother Nature is one fine woman in these regions. She can be wicked, but for the most part she is beautiful.

Tom wrote:

The Tetons are one of the most beautiful places in the world. The hills seem to sing out beautifully to me. If I could come back here, I certainly would.

Jackie reflected on the beauty of Nature during an interview:

We had just got done swimming and it was freezing cold that night. But we came back and we were in Circle, and we thought about the day. And I remember when we were writing in our journal—the beautiful view. Because we were right next to Devil's Tower and you could look up and see the big rock there and the stars were beautiful out there. I remember thinking that if I wasn't such a city girl I'd love to live out there—in that spot, in that camping park. I would love to live there, because it was just so beautiful.

Adrienne wrote:

We went to the Badlands. I was just in awe of them, especially after just waking up. They were like nothing I'd ever seen before. They look like huge sculptures or ancient ruins. There were tons of them too.

Hannah wrote:

When we went to the Black Hills, the beauty of it amazed me. Now I understand more why the land was amazing and sacred to the Native Americans. It looked like it all fit together, like it was painted like a picture. Really it was just layers of sedimentary rocks. And when we first saw Devil's Tower, I almost lost my breath. I had no idea how beautiful it was going to be. From our campsite, we could see it perfectly, when I looked at it with the sunset behind it, it almost took my breath away.

Faith, a student who often struggled with writing, wrote:

When we were driving on the wildlife loop, I thought that was the coolest thing ever. I have never seen wild animals just come up to vehicles like they did. Whenever I see animals it makes me happy because animals have such unique things about them. I think Devil's Tower is amazing, but I just don't get how a rock can form out of the ground like that, but after all it's very beautiful.

The fact that Faith's writing, and her ability to express herself, grew during the trip is also noteworthy. Having taught Faith in English class for a year, I had not seen her exhibit the quality of writing content that she was able to compose during the trip. This causes me to question the impact that outdoor education has on students with learning disabilities or students who struggle with literacy skills. This is an area of research that needs to be explored further.

From a science and history perspective, we noticed that our students' objective journaling and attention to detail increased as well. They often recorded observations that had not been pointed out to them. They would check the altimeter themselves, they would read information on signs and in brochures, and they would synthesize the information and record details. Their ability to use these higher order skills, such as synthesizing, summarizing, and predicting, grew as the trip progressed. As teachers who all require a great deal of writing in our classes, we were excited to see this growth. Experience and hands-on learning produced greater details in student writing, excellent observations, and an increase in higher-level thinking skills. The following journal entries detail this observation.

Darren wrote:

> We headed towards the Medicine Wheel. I noticed that as we climbed the temperature was dropping quickly. It was getting colder and colder...as we approached the clouds in the sky, I also noticed that the plant life was disappearing...becoming smaller. It was about 40 degrees when we arrived.

Margaret wrote:

> We stopped on the side of the road and looked for fossils. I found one too! It was a seashell fossil. The Bighorn Mountains are so beautiful. We are almost 10,000 feet above sea level. Millions of years ago, water covered the mountains. We know that because of the fossils we found—they were seashells.

Greg wrote:

> The land formations seem to change by the mile, which is very cool. The pinnacles on the side of the mountains are amazing and all the trees have disappeared and the sage is back.

Through their writing, students were able to demonstrate an understanding of science based solely on observation. That night at campfire, Randy was able to lead further discussions on how climate impacts landscape.

In addition to nature and hands-on learning inspiring stronger writing, students were also able to reflect and verbalize new knowledge during interviews. Students would often provide great detail about what they had learned. When asked what he liked the best about the program, James replied:

> Just the educational experience, I'd say. Like we got to see everything. We went to Fort Laramie, we got to see the Badlands. The Badlands where you saw how the old settlers had to go through there, and how that would have sucked cuz the land was just wicked. Then we saw the ruts and everything. It was crazy. It was a rock. A big rock. But so many carts went over it. It was probably about six feet deep and that was just from constant carts going over that. So you can get an idea of how many people went down that trail and moved west. Like the decimation of the buffalos. We learned how many there used to be and how many there are today. And we learned about the downfall of the Indians. The rising of the western settlers from Europe. I learned a lot on this trip. And that was an event in itself.

When asked what Greg would remember about the program, he replied:

> The geyser. That was just crystal clear. And that there was a tunnel going down. That just amazed my mind. I don't know how that works. That was amazing... I'd like to come back just to see everything. This land over here is beautiful. The structure of the mountains. Everything about them. I'd take my kids here. It's an experience to see.

Perhaps the most important indicators of increased growth and motivation happened as a result of discovery. In many instances, students discovered new things during walks, or exploration. For example, Angel recalled a moment in the Bighorn Mountains where one student's discovery pulled the rest of the students into the experience. She wrote:

We had to pull over on the mountain road, as far over as we could, as both vans needed to rest the brakes. You, Bauer, and I had gotten out. Bauer said there were probably fossils close to the surface where we were. That dirt and rock were millions to billions of years old. Margaret was the only person that got out of the van, even after all of our coaxing. Then, Margaret found the first fossil. A great shell fossil. As she holds the find into the air and yells, "I found one!!!" other students started filing out of the van like she had just found gold! Sometimes it takes other students to motivate other students. Obviously, what we, as instructors, had to say did not have much bearing on them at that moment. From there, more students found fossils, as did we. A science lesson was born. "What is this?" Again, students were encouraged to go get their fossil sheets and find possible answers to their question. "How did they get way up here?" Ahh, Geography lesson born! "What if this area once had water over it? How was that? Did the mountains grow and push up out of the water or did the water recede as a result of Earth's cyclical cleansing?" Questions prompted more questions and again, learning presented itself with the teaching and learning occurring among students with staff merely facilitating the conversations.

Randy reflected on a student's response to the program, mainly because this student loved nature so much. Randy said:

Every time I saw him, or observed him, he was just beaming. I mean it was just like everything was a new experience. As instructors, all three of us get great enjoyment out of that. It's really neat to see that in a student, because we see so much of the time people that don't pay attention to what's out there and things pass them by and they don't recognize these really cool opportunities.

One instance that both Randy and Angel talked about in interviews involved Faith. Faith was very hesitant to go on the trip. In our alternative school, she did not participate fully in science or history, and rarely smiled or interacted with people she did not know well. During the trip, however, we saw her begin to engage in activities and learning opportunities. It all started with her discovery. She detailed the find in this journal entry:

When we were driving, Amy thought she saw a moose, so we stopped to go check it out and when we were walking, we never saw a moose, but as I was walking I discovered bones and there was lots of bones. We weren't sure what kind of animal it was, but all I know is that it was more than I expected to see. Bauer thinks that the animal was a baby elk, but he's not sure yet. We're going to examine it later today.

What Faith discovered during her walk in the Big Horns was a full skeleton of a small elk. Soon other students crowded around her and she showed her discovery with a huge beaming smile on her face! She led the discussion on identifying the animal as students drew the skeleton and measured bones. She excitedly waited for the opportunity to share her findings once we got to camp, and with more resources was able to properly identify the animal. I wrote in my journal:

> I'm amazed at the transformation in Faith. She was so unsure about coming on this trip and nearly didn't get in the van. But today, she discovered a full skeleton while walking in a meadow looking at wildflowers. She was so excited when she called for us to come and look! I've never seen her this engaged, this motivated, and this excited about learning! She followed the scientific inquiry process, framed great questions, and used the process of elimination to reach her conclusion.

During the 2004 trip, it was the Snake River that provided moments of discovery. After setting up camp, we walked to the river and Mr. Bauer asked, "What do you think the rate of this river is right now?" Since we were white-water rafting the Snake the next day, student interest was high. Students began throwing out guesses. Mr. Bauer then helped students develop an experiment and gave them hints as to how to discover the river rate. Margaret wrote in her journal:

> We went down to the river to see how fast it was moving. Three of us went 100 feet away from everyone else and the rest threw sticks in the water, and the three of us would tell them when the stick passed, so that Mr. Bauer could stop timing. We discovered that the river was traveling about four miles an hour.

Soon four of the boys were working on developing their own experiments. They began creating model rivers and dams along the shore. They hypothesized that dams would slow the river down, but were unsure to what extent the river rate would be impacted. For over an hour, they used timers, created dams, and developed hypotheses and new lines of inquiry. Though they weren't able to come to solid conclusions before nightfall, they were extremely motivated by their exploration of the river.

Spontaneous moments of exploration happened countless times on the trip. Students would try to identify the difference between types of hawks and eagles based on seeing beautiful birds flying overhead. With Randy's help, students set up a population study of a herd of bison discovered along the Custer Wildlife Loop. They interviewed Lakota artists working at the Crazy Horse Memorial and recorded their interview results in their journals. These moments of discovery provided countless educational opportunities for us as teachers.

While students were discovering and exploring nature, they also began exploring new roles as students. Mezirow (2009) writes that the exploration of options for new roles is a phase of transformative learning. For many of our students, turning in schoolwork on time was linked to being a "good" student, but most of them said that they "rarely" ever did it. On the trip, however, students began exploring the option of being a student who turned in work on time. One example of this occurred with the mini-lessons that each student was asked to "teach" to the group. During the 2006 trip, Randy handed out a variety of nonfiction articles to each student and instructed them to "learn the materials" as they would be called upon at any time to be the "teacher of the moment." The articles were on topics that we would have the opportunity to discuss over the next two-days such as altitude sickness, mountain lions, structural geology of the Big Horns, and other science-related topics. We never reminded the students to study or prepare, yet each time that we "called upon" a leader (we planned it so that each assigned topic nicely fit into a stop that we made), they were ready to teach. Some students used notes that they had hand-written, while others spoke from memory. After teaching each of their lessons, they received applause and thanks from their peers. In one note from my journal:

> Greg just beamed today as he presented his lesson on Big Horn geology. He was throwing around science terms like they were a part of his every day language. Everyone listened intensely to his every word. He even asked some quiz questions when he was finished. I told him, "Great job!" after-

wards and he said, "It feels pretty cool to teach once in awhile I guess." I said, "Well, maybe you'll be a teacher or a ranger some day."

"Maybe," he said.

The trip enabled Greg to try on the role of teacher, leader, and facilitator. Before the trip, he claimed that he hated presenting in front of people and that school was always boring. But on the trip he tried out a new role—that of a student who completed assignments, presented well, and became a leader. A few years after the trip Greg and I reconnected and he is currently studying wildlife management. The trip reinforced Greg's love of the outdoors and opened him up to the idea of teaching others.

These positive experiences yield some difficult questions. Though research supports the belief that hands-on learning increases motivation, and our students responded so well to it, why are there such limited opportunities for students to actually experience anything hands-on? Why is outdoor education a rarity in many school settings? Administration often argues that too much risk is involved in outdoor education, yet they do not hesitate to send buses and vans to athletic events all over the country. Transporting students always carries an element of risk, yet our district incorporated safety measures into the plan. For example, our drivers' records needed to be free of any accidents, and the vans we rented had to be provided by our district's transportation service. In regards to camping and wilderness risks, we specifically selected camping at KOA or state campgrounds that were near telephones and ranger stations. Though we trained our students on snake and bear safety, we selected areas to hike and walk that were well traveled. We also carefully met with students who had medical concerns such as diabetes and asthma, and each of our students was required to have a physical prior to the trip. Our school nurse partnered with us prior to the trip, and gave us information on any illnesses students had. In addition, Angel and I had basic first aid certification, and Randy had experiences as an Emergency Medical Technician and wilderness first responder. We also set up a safeguard by having three teachers leading the trips. This enabled a teacher to be with students at all times. Three different groups of hiking, studying, or exploration could be going on simultaneously. Students were told prior to the trip that we would do everything as a family, and that they would be with an adult all the time. By keeping our students busy, and by creating a family environment, we reduced the risks of dangers or students "getting in trouble," which is often a concern of teachers. I do not discount that there is risk involved with providing experiential education programs, but I do believe that proper planning reduces risk and enables students to re-engage in learning.

Other negative arguments include lack of funding for these opportunities. Though it took extra time for us, Angel, Randy and I found private donors willing to partner with us. Fundraising became easier each year, as donors continued the relationship with us. In addition, we kept costs low by traveling light, cooking our own food, and camping. We also partnered with businesses to provide discounts on camping supplies and used our own supplies from home when necessary.

Additional arguments against outdoor or hands-on learning involve taking time away from a set curriculum to teach new skills. Angel, Randy, and I worked to make sure that the curriculum aligned with state and district standards and received approval from the school district's curriculum director and superintendent. During the trip, students were often working on state outcome packets, writing notes for papers, or conducting interviews with park rangers. All of this information was then brought back to school and a post-trip workday was set up so that students could synthesize information and complete any additional requirements.

Further arguments against experiential education might be that only a small number of students are reached through these programs. Successful programs, however, spread. Students returned each year excited to share their experiences with other teachers and peers. In our school, other programs began to develop and a new team of teachers led trips in 2007 and 2009. In addition, returning students often became leaders in the building. They began serving on committees, joining organizations, and modeling success to others. Students also promoted the program through conversations with financial donors, parents, and district office staff. Though only a small number of students actually participated, a large number of people were impacted by the success of the program and the passion of the teachers and students.

All of the concerns and arguments need to be addressed before starting a program, and research results from relevant studies like these can help facilitate understanding about the benefits of hands-on learning and outdoor education. Through student interviews and teacher and student journals it is clear that our alternative students were motivated by hands-on learning and felt that they learned more because they were experiencing history and science firsthand. They felt that traveling away from home helped eliminate outside influences. In addition, students showed an increase in academic achievement. For example, student writing became more descriptive and included imagery and relevant high-level questions, and all students passed quizzes with 90% or above. Spontaneous discoveries also sparked interest and motivation. And most importantly, students disengaged with learning communities became transformed and excited about gathering new knowledge, and built positive relationships with both staff and students. The importance of creating a sense of belonging and fostering positive relationships and transformative learning through dialogue will be discussed in the next chapter.

CHAPTER THREE

Restoring Community: The Impact of Restorative Justice Circles on Student Feelings of Connectedness

There is much evidence that adolescents and youth who are disconnected from mainstream institutions and opportunities are likely to suffer significant, often long-term, negative effects as they enter adulthood. Many of these youth may reconnect to education and/or identify ways they can be productive and creative if given the opportunity to do so through alternative education strategies and settings. (Zwieg, 2003, p. 10)

School Connectedness

In addition to concerns about student engagement and motivation, something is lacking in our current educational system, especially when focusing on students who struggle through high school. As students grow older, they feel less attached to school (McNeely, Nonnemaker, and Blum, 2002, p. 146). By high school as many as 40–60% of students become chronically disengaged (Klem and Connell, 2004, p. 262). And for those students who fail to "fit in" to traditional education systems, there is an even greater disconnect; at-risk students feel even less of a sense of belonging in conventional classrooms (Beck and Malley, 1998). This is a major concern because connectedness has been linked to higher levels of engagement, and lower levels of stress, violence, suicide attempts and drug use (Blum and Libbey, 2004, p. 231). Because of these concerns, a strategy that re-engaged our alternative students was using restorative justice Talking Circles to rebuild connectedness.

In order to discuss the impact of Circles on feelings of connectedness, it is first important to discuss the term "connectedness." There are many different definitions of school connectedness (Libbey, 2004, p. 274). The terms "school bonding," "school climate," and "school connectedness," all reference student-teacher relationships, feelings of support, and a sense of belonging (Libbey, 2004, p. 274). School connectedness consists of two primary and interdependent components: attachment, characterized by close relationships, and commitment, characterized by investment in school (Catalano, Haggerty, Oesterle, Fleming, and Hawkins, 2004, p. 252). Researchers also study safety, creative engagement, and meaningful roles (Whitlock, 2006). Critical requirements for connectedness include students experiencing high academic expectations and support, positive adult-student relationships, and physical and emotional safety (Wingspread, 2004). For the purpose of measuring the impact of restorative justice Circles on our students, I will be focusing on feelings of support, student-teacher relationships, and a sense of belonging. I will be using the term "school connectedness."

When speaking of support, it is important to realize that support should be felt by all students, with no one being pushed aside (te Riele, 2006, p. 67). The belief by students that adults in school care about them as individuals, not just as a student body, is a major component of school connectedness (Blum & Libbey, 2004, p. 231). These feelings of support are linked to academic competence, fewer behavioral problems and higher levels of engagement (Klem & Connell, 2004; Murray, 2002; Pianta, 1999).

Teachers and adults within schools are key contributors to making students feel known. Student-teacher relationships matter. Fostering caring student-teacher relationships by creating opportunities to learn about students' needs, histories and cultures has been linked to closing the achievement gap (Bernard, 2004). As stated by Cassidy and Bates (2005), students see their teachers' respect for them as key to their success at school (p. 89). Creating trusting relationships between students and teachers and ensuring that students feel close to at least one supportive adult are effective strategies for increasing connectedness. (Wingspread Declaration, 2004). According to Perez (2000):

> Teacher caring is important because it encourages student commitment to school and their engagement in learning. It can be a source of motivation for all students, but especially for culturally diverse students who may be at risk of failing or who may be disengaged from schooling. A lack of connec-

tion is often a consequence of feeling "invisible" or anonymous in the school setting. (p. 102)

This is an important factor when working with students who have often been labeled "at-risk," such as the poor or students of color (Deschenes, Tyack, & Cuban, 2001, ¶ 52–54). Poor student-teacher relationships may even lead to dropping out of school altogether. In research on "excluded students," teacher-student relationship problems accounted for a common reason for a permanent disconnection with school (Pomeroy, 1999, p. 466). In contrast, positive teacher-student relationships may help reduce social inequities by creating alternative situations that disrupt cycles of inequality (Bernard, 2004; Cummins, 1986).

Along with feeling supported and having a bond with a caring adult, student connectedness is also tied to a sense of belonging. The psychological sense that one belongs in a classroom is linked to successful learning (Beck & Malley, 1998, 133).

Additionally, Beck and Malley (1998) argue, "Most children fail in school not because they lack the necessary cognitive skills, but because they feel detached, alienated, and isolated from others and from the educational process" (p. 133). Providing settings where students learn about caring affects their feelings of social connectedness and is linked to dropout prevention (Rauner, 2000, p. 78).

In addition to feeling connected to school and school staff, students need to feel connected to each other. When they don't, negative peer relationships lead to dropping out of school in high school years (Wentzel & Caldwell, 1997). On the other hand, "positive group membership has been a consistent predictor of young adolescents' academic achievement when other aspects of peer relationships are taken into account" (Wentzel & Caldwell, 1997, p. 1208). Jennings (2003) writes, "Peer relationships are also significant influences on identification with school as well as with academic achievement" (p. 46).

We knew that we needed a central space where we could build feelings of connectedness, so we used Talking Circles as a tool for promoting dialogue. Taylor (2009) writes that dialogue in a trusting environment fosters transformative learning. He writes:

Dialogue becomes the medium for critical reflection to be put into action, where experience is reflected on, assumptions and beliefs are questioned, and habits of mind are ultimately transformed. The dialogue is not so much analytical, point-counterpoint dialogue, but dialogue emphasizing relational and trustful communication, often at times "highly personal and self-disclosing." (p. 9)

This was true for our group. During Circle the questions that we framed were not meant to inspire debate, rather they asked students to turn inward. We had opportunities for debate or counterpoint styles of dialogue during mini-lessons or while in the vans. The questions asked in Circle differed from those asked during daily lessons. For example during our visit to Badlands National Park we asked, "Should national parks limit the number of visitors allowed to hike or climb here?" Students were then able to voice their opinions and listen to counterarguments. At Circle that night, however, we framed the question a different way asking, "What was significant about today's visit to Badlands National Park? What stood out for you?" Students were then offered time to reflect inwardly before sharing their thoughts with others. More information about how we framed questions for Circle will be shared later in the chapter.

Along with creating safe places for dialogue to occur, Taylor (2009) writes that establishing authentic relationships with students fosters transformative learning. When relationships are solidly built on trust and respect students feel more open to sharing. Taylor writes:

It is through building trusting relationships that learners develop the confidence to deal with learning on an affective level, where transformation at times can be perceived as threatening and an emotionally charged experience. (p. 13)

As this chapter details, time spent in Circle changed student perceptions of us as teachers. We became more human in their eyes, which allowed a great sense of trust and confidence. Our knowledge of our students as individual human beings grew and we were able to respond to their full humanity. All of this was possible because of our time spent in Circle.

This chapter attempts to study restorative justice Circles in an experiential context as an alternative strategy to promote feelings of connectedness and relatedness and to foster transformative learning with alternative high school students. In order to lead into Circle research, one must first study the background of restorative justice.

Restorative Justice Overview

Peacemaking Circles have grown in popularity due to their connection within the restorative justice movement (Coates, Umbreit and Vos, 2003). In addition, the idea has grown in support through the United Nation's Economic and Social Council, which adopted a resolution encouraging member states to use mediation and restorative justice to promote democratic principles of individual and community responsibility (Varnham, 2005, p. 88).

Restorative justice is an "alternative approach to criminal justice" that began evolving in the United States about fifteen years ago in response to the ineffectiveness of our current justice system (Pranis, 2005). As defined by Varnham (2005), restorative justice "describes a response to wrongdoing which focuses on people and relationships rather than on punishment and retribution" (p. 91). Restorative justice grew from concerns that some needs were not being addressed in the traditional justice system; it brings victim and offender together in a conferencing process to promote healing (Zehr, 2002, p. 13). The victim and offender meet, each bringing family members or friends as supporters, and, led by a Circle Keeper, they discuss their feelings surrounding the offense. The offender is held accountable for his or her actions, but is also encouraged and supported by the members of the Circle community (Zehr, 2002, p. 17). Instead of punishing in isolation, the offender is encouraged through transformation and is given the opportunity to make amends. According to Susan Sharpe (1998), five key principles guide restorative justice. These are:

1. Restorative justice invites full participation and consensus
2. Restorative justice seeks to heal what is broken, not only for the victim but also for the offender

3. Restorative justice seeks to make the offender fully and directly accountable, by not only facing up to his/her offending but by confronting those who have suffered as a result
4. Restorative justice seeks to reunite what has been divided
5. Restorative justice seeks to strengthen the community in order to prevent further harm (pp. 7–12)

Indeed, the community plays an essential role in restorative justice. It is the community that serves to communicate beyond law and regulation and into the world of feelings and expectations. According to Pranis (2005), the following three steps are established community steps in working with juvenile offenders:

1. Provide feedback about the impact of the offender's action on others
2. Reinforce a sense of value and intrinsic worth of the offender
3. Acknowledge pain in the offender's life without excusing behavior

Restorative Justice in Schools

In the 1990s, a systemic effort to use Circles in public processes grew out of work in the Yukon, Canada (Pranis, 2005, p. 8). Varnham (2003) argues that due to school safety concerns, high numbers of suspensions and expulsions and the quest to promote democracy in education, it was only logical that restorative justice began being used in schools. Hopkins (2002) describes a paradigm shift from retributive justice in schools in which misbehavior should be punished, to a restorative approach involving dialogue, support and mediation in which the "misbehaving" student is allowed to choose a path that restores harm. The potential for repairing harms and reducing recidivism among school offenders was something that interested teachers and administrators. For example, Circles in Minnesota began as part of the criminal justice process, but were soon used in schools (Pranis, 2004). Through grants, school administrators and teachers were trained in the Circle process. As Walker (2001) writes:

It can become a school's standard conflict resolution practice when an offender admits misbehavior. It is a process that can teach empathy and problem solving skills. Additionally, it teaches that those most affected by wrongdoing can come together in a positive way to work toward repairing harm. (p. 7)

In Minnesota, Nancy Riestenberg, a prevention specialist with the Minnesota Department of Children, Families and Learning, was an advocate for the use of restorative justice. During an evaluation after three years of its implementation, she noticed changes in the Minnesota schools that were utilizing restorative justice:

> In one building in particular there were very strong quantitative results. It appears that with the institution of Circles to Repair Harm, along with circles used in the classroom for building community, they went from about seven incidents of violence a day to around one a day in the course of three-and-a-half years. That was a significant drop. There was also a significant drop over three years in terms of overall behavior referrals to the office. They went from somewhere in the thousands to 450, like 1600 to 450 over the course of three years. (Mirsky, 2003, ¶ 8)

According to the MN Restorative Justice Grants Final Report, alternative schools, including ours, were using restorative justice in the following ways:

1. Weekly, daily or homeroom classroom circles: used as a means of connecting with students and to build community and creating a positive school climate
2. Students reported that they learned social skills: how to listen, how to talk respectfully, how to respect people who think or believe differently from yourself
3. Circles to repair harm: set up when students broke rules or caused harm. Fewer training participants reported using the process to repair harm, as that is a more difficult process. However, as the result of restorative measures training, individual schools reported significant changes in the way that they handled discipline.

4. Study Circles and Writing Circles: teachers would send around a talking piece to solicit responses from all students to questions or to conduct creative writing groups

5. Relapse circles: a recovery high school used the circle for students who violate the sobriety requirement of the academy.

6. Staff circles around administrator challenges, staff issues with leadership and each other. (Riestenberg, 2003)

In addition to use in Minnesota schools, restorative justice Circles are being used in public schools in New Zealand and the UK. In New Zealand, an emphasis on community partnerships is apparent, as schools utilize community elders, parents, families, coaches, and other supporters of youth (Wearmouth, 2007, p. 44). In New Zealand, the aims of restorative practices in schools are:

• Address the problem
• Encourage understanding of the effects of the offense on all individuals involved and on the school community
• Invite the taking up of responsibility
• Avoid creating shame and blame
• Promote the healing of hurt
• Open up avenues of redress
• Restore working relationships
• Include everyone in the community envisioned by the process rather than divide people into insider and outside groups (Wearmouth, 2007, p. 40)

Despite promising evidence, restorative justice in schools has not been an easy addition. In many cases, scheduling does not allow teachers, students, and principals to meet for Circle in a timely manner. Furthermore, scheduling time for family and community members is difficult. It is a process that takes time and dedication (Rourke, 2001, p. 3). Hopkins (2002) acknowledges this, but states, "Shortage of time for training, ongoing support and review are real issues, but again I have found that, once convinced, a school finds time and funds for the initiative and can be creative in finding time for the training" (p. 148). Indeed, many trained teachers have begun to use the Circle process within their classrooms to build community and to promote democratic processes of decision-making.

The Origin of Peacemaking Circles

A key element in restorative justice, and in our summer school program, was time spent in Circle. "Whatever your cultural or ethnic background your ancestors probably sat in circle," writes Greg Lewis (2002, p. 2), a teacher who uses Circles in his classrooms. Other authors (Baldwin, 1994) state that the use of Circles for communication and problem solving is as ancient as humankind. Most Circle practitioners (Boyes-Watson, 2008; Pranis, 2005; Zehr, 2002; Baldwin, 1998) credit indigenous cultures for the Circle process. Circles were traditional means for solving problems and were based on the principles of the medicine wheel (Boyes-Watson, 2005). Pranis (2005) writes, "Such processes still exist among indigenous people around the world, and we are deeply indebted to those who have kept these practices alive as a source of wisdom and inspiration for modern Western cultures" (p. 7). The training that Angel, Randy and I received through the Minnesota Department of Education has its roots with the Tlingit First Nation people of the Yukon Territory in Northwestern Canada. Other programs originate in other cultures such as the restorative justice Circles used in New Zealand public schools. These Circles are influenced by traditional Maori cultural values (Wearmouth, 2007). When utilizing any indigenous process, an awareness of history, background, and proper use is important. Carolyn Boyes-Watson, a sociologist and Circle researcher, writes that "The peacemaking Circle was given to Westerners by Indigenous individuals who were willing not only to share the wisdom of their ancestors but also to do so with a culture that has all but destroyed their precious heritage" (Boyes-Watson, 2008, p. 12). Experiential education has often inadvertently used processes from Native cultures in an incorrect manner (Couch & Hall, 1992). Research on the topic is difficult to find, but an awareness of care concerning the use of these processes

is important. Angel, Randy and I were fortunate to have quality train-
ers to guide us through the process.

Philosophy of Circles

Circle is a process that uses structural elements to bring people together. Pranis (2005) argues that the structure does not limit participation; instead, it allows participants the freedom to speak truthfully
and to drop the masks and barriers that individuals carry outside the
Circle space (p. 11). The underlying philosophy of Circles acknowledges that we are all in need of community and help from others, and
in turn, that we all have something to offer other human beings (p. 6).
The fact that participants sit in a circle form symbolizes shared leadership, equality, connection, and inclusion (p. 11).

Much of the Circle philosophy has to do with respect, empowerment, and equality. Greenwood (2005) says, "While Circles vary
somewhat in style and structure, they all seek to cultivate a climate of
mutual respect and caring that is value-oriented and heart-based, that
engages the emotions as well as the mind" (p. 2). The Circle process
allows all present to have an equal opportunity to speak without in-
terruptions (Umbreit, 2003, ¶ 1). Rather than conversations that go
back and forth, the passing of a talking piece fosters reflective listening and safety (Umbreit, 2003, ¶ 1). Circle is empowering because it
gives every participant a chance to be deeply heard. All participants
are able to speak, yet can choose to pass and remain silent. Voices that
are often silenced, such as youth voices, suddenly have a safe place to
speak. Boyes-Watson (2002) states:

> The circle process opens a space where young people are able to speak and
> be heard. The experience of being respectfully and fully listened to is one of
> the most profoundly meaningful elements of the circle process. In an adult-
> dominated world, young people are marginalized and voiceless; disadvan-
> taged young people are especially "voiceless" at home, in school and in the
> wider community. The circle process offers an opportunity for participation
> as equals that does not exist in any other social context. (p. 13)

There are a wide variety of reasons to use Circles. At the basic level, Circles build community. According to Pranis, Stuart, and Wedge (2003):

> Circles bring us together to share who we are beyond our appearances. They're places of listening—of hearing what it's like to be someone else. They're also places for being heard—for expressing what's on our minds and hearts and having others receive it deeply. (p. 3)

The Circle Process is a storytelling process (Pranis, 2005, p. 4). Stories unite people, help people empathize with one another, and help people learn from each other (Pranis, 2005). Story also creates a world of invitation where people are simultaneously listening to another person and reviewing their own memories at the same time, leading to the formation of connection (Baldwin, 2005, p. 7). By inviting honest storytelling in a structured space, strangers can become united. This process has been used to unite people in the United States for many generations and through various programs. Highlander Workshops in the South in the 1960s used learning circles to promote storytelling so that participants could analyze and learn from experiences of other group members (Horton, 1998). Weekly Circles are held at the Smokey House Center, a program for troubled youth, in Vermont (Rauner, 2000). Through PeerSpirit, women come together through outdoor adventure and Circle (Baldwin, 1998). Circles are also being used as learning circles in professional development on college campuses and in educational settings (Collay, Dunlap, Enloe, and Gagnon, 1998).

Circles can also be used for specific purposes such as relationship development, healing, community building, and restorative justice efforts (Boyes-Watson, 2002). Different types of Circles are used for different purposes. Types of Circles include: Talking, Understanding, Healing, Sentencing, Support, Community-Building, Conflict, Reintegration, and Celebration (Pranis, 2005).

Components of a Talking Circle

Because there are many different types of Peacemaking Circles used today, I need to describe the specific restorative justice process used by Randy, Angel, and me. Our primary type of Circle used was the Talking Circle. In Talking Circles, a question can be explored and many different voices can be heard (Pranis, 2005). Talking Circles consist of four key components: a Circle Keeper, the guidelines, the talking piece, and the introductory ceremony (Pranis, Stuart, and Wedge, 2003, p. 141).

The Circle Keeper is the facilitator of the Circle. The role of the Circle Keeper is to prepare for the Circle by establishing the place, inviting participants, planning the introductory ceremony, and guiding the process. The Circle Keeper is not the person who runs the Circle; instead, he/she serves the Circle and its participants (Pranis, Stuart, and Wedge, 2003, p. 84). The Circle Keeper sits within the Circle and participates as an equal. In fact, in all Circles all participants are equal no matter the age, job title, or circumstance that brought the Circle together (Greenwood, 2005, ¶ 2). Though all are equal, it is the responsibility of the Circle Keeper to be focused and organized and to ensure that Circle guidelines are being followed (Coates, Umbreit, and Vos, 2003, p. 270).

Guidelines are the norms that are set up by the group prior to beginning. Some guidelines are established parts of the Circle process, whereas others are more specific. The key values guiding the Circle usually include the following:

1. Circle is a place for respectful listening
2. Circle participation is voluntary
3. Each individual has an equal opportunity to participate
4. Individuals should enter Circle with an open heart and mind
5. Circle is a sacred space
6. Circle is confidential (Coates, Umbreit, and Vos, 2003, p. 268)

If a Circle feels out of sync, a keeper or other participant may bring the focus back to the values or guidelines.

The talking piece is a key component of the Circle process. The talking piece is passed around the Circle, permitting equal participation. The talking piece is usually selected by the Circle Keeper and is often a special item that is meaningful to the community, or a natural object such as a shell, rock or feather (Pranis, 2005). Whoever holds the talking piece is invited to speak, while all other members of the circle are actively listening. When a speaker is finished speaking, he/she passes the talking piece on to the person sitting directly next to him/her. The passing follows the path of the Circle and does not skip any participant. Participants may pass and choose not to speak (Lewis, 2003, p. 2). Benefits to the talking piece include the promotion of dialogue, the development of listening skills, and the focus on promoting equality (Pranis, Stuart, and Wedge, 2003, p. 100). In addition, the talking piece slows everything down. The pace of a Circle is different from that of other discussions.

Circles usually begin with a ritual or ceremony. Sometimes a poem is read. Sometimes a chime signals the start of the Circle. The opening of Circle varies depending on the purpose (Coates, Umbreit, and Vos, 2003, p. 268). In many instances, Circle Keepers refer to an item set within the center of the Circle, such as a quilt, painting, poster with words, or a significant object selected by the group. In the case of our trips, the campfire serves as our center. In the case of the evening without fire, the orange light of the lamp took its place.

Because all Circles serve different purposes, and all Circle Keepers have different styles, it is important to explore the way that Angel, Randy, and I facilitate Circle. First, as previously stated, each of us is in charge of planning Circle on a designated evening. We each pack many diverse readings, and journal topics so that we are prepared to respond to a variety of topics, moods, or tones. We reflect on our day, read the mood of our group, and make a selection prior to Circle—individually, we are all very flexible and only once or twice regenerate a particularly effective opening from trip to trip. Usually, the person who is Circle Keeper will have a brief moment to get ready, while the other instructors will be journaling with students and tending the fire. We trust in the expertise of each other, and on the evenings when we aren't facilitating Circle, we are participating as a student would. We truly believe in equality in Circle, and often share just as much as our students. We cry as they cry, we laugh as they laugh. Our collective style is one of openness and welcome. As instructors, we also never interrupt and honor the Talking Piece. As students review the day and the curriculum, they may have misspoken about historical facts; however, we never interrupt or correct during Circle. Instead, we make a mental note, jot it in our journals, and reteach concepts the next day. We look forward to the time just as much as our students. The level of openness and community serve as a tool to rejuvenate our Spirits. The following interview results will shed light on why these moments are so effective.

Causes of School Disconnection

When analyzing the impact of Circle on feelings of connectedness, it is first important to establish why students felt disconnected from school. From my interviews with eleven Westward Bound students for this chapter on Circles, it became clear that disconnection played a major role in their placement at an alternative school. To discover what happened in their pasts, I initially asked, "What situations in your educational past caused you to feel disconnected from school?" It is highly significant that nine out of eleven students immediately pointed to student-teacher relationships.

One way that students felt disconnected was they felt that they were just a number to their teachers. Jackie, a seventeen-year-old, reflected on her previous experiences in a mainstream school:

> Most of the things were from my mainstream school. The teachers didn't really have a connection with you because there are so many students and they really didn't talk to you. They just gave you your homework and did the stuff on the board and that was it.

Adrienne, a sixteen-year-old, recalled a similar experience:

> When I was in mainstream school, I just didn't know the teachers. They didn't care. We were just a name on the attendance list. They just got paid

for the time they were there. They didn't care how good of an education we got.

This idea that teachers were just doing a job and getting paid was mentioned again by Clyde, an eighteen-year-old, who believed negative student-teacher relationships were his primary reason for feeling disconnected with school prior to moving to an alternative setting:

> To me, I feel like teachers don't really know how you feel in the mainstream school compared to an alternative school—you get a lot closer to them. And they seem to care about you a lot more than just teaching you, or getting paid, or making you sit there and do your work.

Other students were even more specific and recalled situations where they perceived teachers as being purposely hurtful. Faith, an eighteen-year-old, recalls:

> The teachers were always really mean to me. Before I came here to alternative school, the teachers were really, really rude.

Guy recalled his early experiences with this:

> Well, when I was in elementary school I thought a few of my teachers were mean. When I was younger, I was shy about raising my hand and asking for help.

Though Guy inadvertently connected mean teachers with being shy and not getting help, three other students pointed directly to teachers not helping them. Hannah remembered the exact grade that this feeling began:

> When I was younger I had a third grade teacher who whenever I asked questions would kind of ridicule me like it was a dumb question to ask. When I fell really behind, I kind of just quit asking for help. It just all seemed kind of pointless.

Clyde felt that teachers did not believe that he actually needed help:

> In a mainstream school I tried to tell them that I didn't understand work, they must not have believed me or must have just thought I was slackin', but I didn't understand any of it.

Suzy recalled frustration transitioning into middle school:

> And to hear that, like, in some situations where I got help in elementary school for things, and then I got to middle school and the help stopped. They just basically said that I wasn't "dumb enough." So, that was one way that I got disconnected from the school environment.

These feelings of frustration and alienation from teachers were often felt immediately. Sheila, an eighteen-year-old who recently changed districts, recalled a first impression of a teacher that left her feeling disconnected:

> Well, I remember my first day of school, I walked into a teacher's room and had headphones on and she was like, "Take off your headphones." And I said, "Class hasn't even started yet." And she said, "You can just leave then." I was just like, "O.k." and I turned them off. That gave me a sour attitude towards her.

For these students, disengagement and feelings of disconnectedness due to teacher action or inaction happened quickly and were vividly recalled. What does this say about our traditional schools? First, it is important to note that most students in the United States are brought up transitioning from elementary to secondary levels. For some of the students interviewed, the close connection with elementary teachers, and the belief that they were cared about and known as a person dissolved upon entering middle and high school. Though the block system and specialty subject areas being taught by high quality staff are deemed necessary in today's secondary schools, what is happening to student feelings of connection with teachers? Serious consideration of transition programs from elementary to secondary school is needed, not temporary bandages that help students adjust, but full systems of permanent support introduced during the physical time of transition that remains in place throughout secondary high school.

What impact does a smaller class size have on feelings of connectedness experienced by youth labeled "at-risk"? Based on student responses, teacher attitude came up often, whereas smaller class size was never mentioned. For these students, a willingness to help, a desire to know students personally, and an attitude that said, "I am here because I want to be, not because I am paid to be," seemed to be important to their perception of student-teacher relationships. In her book, *Other People's Children*, Delpit (1995) echoes the students' statements, "If we do not have some knowledge of children's lives outside of the realms of paper-and-pencil work, and even outside of their classrooms, then we cannot know their strengths" (p. 173). This is true especially when working with students who are culturally different from the teacher. Though more and more teacher workshops focus on discipline, classroom management, and high-stakes test results, very few workshops about current schooling climate focus on ways to build connectedness through teacher attitude. Sometimes connectedness workshops are thrown into prevention and safety columns, but how much training are classroom teachers receiving on the impact of action, word, and inaction on the possibilities of long-term student disengagement? Because the students interviewed said that teachers had such a huge impact on their disconnection from school, I feel that more strategies need to be taught to teachers so that connectedness activities are part of teacher training.

Though having negative student-teacher relationships was the most consistent answer given as to why students experienced feelings of disconnection, a few recalled negative relationships with peers, but as a secondary response.

Suzy said:

A lot of times, like, they would make fun of me because of how my Dad is. He's in a wheelchair, so they made fun of me. "Oh, your Dad's stupid" or "you're gonna be just like him." Or they just say like stuff about me being overweight or just by my looks or what I believed in. And it just made me feel really bad about who I am.

Sheila, an African American who moved to a largely Caucasian neighborhood, attributed moving and peer harassment to her feelings of disconnection:

> Moving made me feel disconnected. My boyfriend and I broke up and he was the only person that I really talked to, so it was weird not having him there anymore. So, I really didn't know how to talk to people and how to go about making friends. And I was cheerleading and I got a lot of crap from being the only black cheerleader. And people were like, "What are you doing here?" And so I just kind of closed myself off from everyone because of the negative experience.

Hannah recalled feelings of alienation that led to disengagement:

> Basically people in my other schools...I didn't really have many friends. The only friend I had was my cousin. She didn't go to the same school as me.

Additionally, one student, Adrienne, spoke of cliques leading to a disconnection with school:

> Yeah, well like when you're in a big school and there's all those little cliques. I definitely did. Like here, everybody talks to everybody, but there....there were certain people that you just wouldn't hang out with. You have your own little group of friends. I didn't like it.

Though bullying and teasing, cliques, and a sense of alienation from friends were mentioned as leading to disconnection, it was student-teacher relationships that students spoke of the most. This is amazing to me, because it shows such resilience within these students. Though these students have faced great challenges in their lives such as poverty, loss of one or both parents, addiction, teen pregnancy, and moving through the foster care system, students only briefly mentioned those challenges and did not tie them to school disconnection. Even when a student mentioned life challenges, she quickly praised the positive teachers in her life now:

> Well, in the past, I had lots of family issues so I didn't get to go to school very often cuz I was always watching my little brother. And that's when drugs entered my life and everything. Now that I have teachers that actually

believe in me and believe that I can do better I actually go to school now. I know that just cuz problems are in my life I can move on and do better.

Clearly, student-teacher relationships, both negative and positive, have a huge impact on alternative students' feelings of connectedness with school.

Circle Fosters Positive Student-Teacher Relationships

When asked if students' perceptions changed about staff or students as a result of Circle, almost every student spoke of teachers first. Though I had perceived that I was close to a few of the students prior to the trip, students spoke at length of Circle as a means to build connection with Angel, Randy, and me. In Circle we teachers honored the Circle foundations of equality, and though we led the ritual and framed the questions, we participated honestly and openly in our responses. Though topics were preplanned, our responses were based on our feelings in that moment. This did not go unnoticed. Faith spoke of time in Circle helping her see her teachers as human beings:

> Yeah. Like we became way closer. I felt like I could actually open up to them and tell them... and tell them how I really felt about the situation...it gives you different perspective of a teacher.

When asked to elaborate, she replied:

> Cuz. You...cuz, you realize that they are not just a teacher...they are a friend also. Someone you can just sit there and talk to about how your day's going, without having to talk about school and homework and stuff.

Adrienne agreed and spoke of feeling equal to her teachers in Circle:

> I learned to think of them more as people than teachers. I did coming here, but even more so after being in Circle and seeing them as one of us. We were all equal.

Jackie spoke of finding the humanness in her teachers as well:

You guys seemed more human...not, like, you know teachers. (Laughs) Sorry, but. Umm. It gives you a level of connection that you don't normally just find in a school...That you don't normally find anywhere.

One thing that Randy, Angel, and I did in Circle was allow all the students to express themselves without interruption or "teacher guidance." We guided students into poems or readings, but once the talking piece began to circle we participated as a member of the Circle space, not leaders. We offered no critiques or feedback. We shared our emotions and thoughts around the day or around the question posed. We became *co-learners* (Freire, 1970). Cranton (2006) describes *co-learners* in transformative learning. She states, "He or she works with learners and tries to find out about their lives and experiences even as learners may be questioning their values. When this happens, students become co-teachers, and knowledge is being created collaboratively" (p. 107). Indeed, I felt that I was learning from my students, just as they were learning from me. For example, during Circle they would often speak of things that they saw that day that I perhaps didn't notice or they would find connections between things that astounded me. Students recognized this role as *co-learner* and it changed their perceptions of us. When asked if her perception of teachers changed as a result of Circle, Suzy spoke of a deep connection as well:

I feel it did. I feel it changed a whole lot. (Pause) The only relationships I'd ever had with teachers were when they were being critical of my work in class or something like that. To just hear them say how much they appreciate me as a person, instead of like what I do in school.

Jackie also brought up getting to know her teachers better:

I fell in love with all three of you guys. Cuz. You guys are just so sweet and you cared about us and you taught us so much. I don't know. All you guys changed. We got to know about your personal lives too. You guys seemed like the students too, I guess. You guys were just friends.

A few students discussed the notion of Circle fostering student-teacher friendships. I asked Angel Salathe about this idea of "friendship" in an e-mail interview. She responded:

I believe that the ancient tradition and practice of Circle had the affect on the students because we created and encouraged a time of sharing around an age old element that has brought people together since man was able to walk. Due to this positive and open space of sharing we created, we allowed ourselves to be 13 human beings, individuals, without labels/titles to share our inner-most selves with one another in a space that was safe to do so. This is the ultimate goal of a Circle... any Circle. For us to create an environment in which the students could see us all as equals, a Circle in which no idea or thought was a dumb one, rather a gift for the other 12 people surrounding the person who spoke. We created a space for the students to feel close to us, to open up to us, a space and an opportunity that our society and traditional/mainstream educational system does not give them.

Because the idea of friendship among students and teachers often has a negative tone in today's educational models, I asked Angel to address the ideas of boundaries and student-teacher friendships. She said:

In today's society and education system, people are too afraid to allow the "friendship" aspect between youth and adult authority figure to happen. What is often misunderstood is that with solid boundaries in place, the student can still feel as though they have a "friend" in us (the teacher), but that can be a one-way street. As an adult, I do not need to have the student be my friend, but I can create an open space for them to feel friendship with me if the correct boundaries are in place. At the end of the day, students will still know I am the teacher, the one calling the shots, but if they follow the rules and adhere to the boundaries I have in place, they can have a voice in those shots.

As teachers, we observed that though students reported feelings of student-teacher friendship, they never questioned our roles as instructors. The Circle somehow facilitated feelings of friendship, but did not take away our "instructor authority"; rather it enhanced student trust in us.

Guy also spoke directly of how Circle helped shift his perspective of teachers:

I didn't expect you guys to be so laid back. I thought, I thought you and Salathe weren't gonna be that nice. And I knew Bauer. It was nice to get along. I can talk to you teachers. It was the only three teachers I'd spent a week with outside of school—outside of my regular life.

With this line of questioning, it is important to note that though the question was directly about Circle, student answers encompassed experiences of teachers throughout the trip.
Guy notes:

> You three teachers were really into this trip. And it all excited us kids to know that everyone—we all wanted to learn about it—it gave us all the same amount of respect for each other.

Clyde seemed to agree that the trip itself impacted his perception:

> Clyde: But even being just with the teachers, it was different. Just the way they acted towards us and around each other.
>
> Amy: In what way?
>
> Clyde: Being so happy. Not, ah, getting frustrated here or there but being more happy. Knowing that we're all together having fun.

Clyde also spoke of learning from teacher-teacher relationships:

> Seeing the way you guys were so happy together. The first day or the first week, I was really just happy to go on the trip to get the credits. I didn't care about meeting people or doing whatever this and that. But the way you guys, Salathe, Bauer, and Amy, connected was unreal. Like, amazing to watch. Even when we were at the wheel, up at the top of the mountain, it was just different to see teachers actually interact like that. Not knowing the experiences that they've already had together, rather than being in school and seeing them in the cafeteria together laughing, it's not, nothin' near like that.

Clyde's response is interesting because perhaps it shows that Angel, Randy, and my feelings of connectedness to each other served as a positive model for our students to follow. When we began our trips, Randy, Angel, and I did not know each other nearly as well as we do now. We all believed deeply in Circle, in our curriculum, in experiential education, in each other, and in our students. We were also deeply connected over similar feelings of nature and humanity. Any slight disagreements regarding maps and when to make dinner, rolled off, as our foundation together was solid. Randy believes that our connection to the earth, and our connection to each other, grounded that. He said:

> We have a background grounded in spirituality, grounded in love and re- spect for the earth, that started when we were really, really little—caring for the earth. I think we are good complements… Coming from a similar way to believe about the earth, that's a major part. And then we pull from that our areas of expertise. As instructors, we were grounded in something before… When students realize that…this is a trilogy. 'They know what they're talk- ing about. They believe what they are talking about. They're not just blow- ing each other off.' That is powerful. That is very powerful that they…that we are rock solid about how we feel about stuff. And that is significant. And that's what pulls them in. There's no crack in the armor. Cuz these kids are so perceptive. They see phoniness and pretending and all that. They've seen patronization all their lives. And anybody that's marginalized hates that. "Just live with me and be with me." The students knew where all of us were coming from. And that leads to a lot of trust and that leads to openness. Kids, no matter how weird a teacher is, come to a conclusion that they are for real. With that, and once they establish that trust with all of us, they real- ize that, "Yeah, these people are for real. This is what they believe in. This ain't a bunch of B.S. Now we're gonna do Circle? Well, yeah, I believe in you, so of course we're gonna do Circle." So we pulled them in.

In addition, we all had fond memories of important Circles in our own lives prior to these trips. I recalled many wonderful campfires and Circles that I experienced during my years as a camp counselor. Randy Bauer also recalls positive feelings of Circle, which he shared with me during a face-to-face interview:

> My background is sitting around thousands of campfires, working at YMCA camps, working with Indian youth, working with at-risk youth, working with the public as a ranger, as a National Park Ranger, working as a Voy- ager at National Parks, bringing skiers into an area where you have a teepee and a fire going…when I hear the word "circle," to me, that brings back all those experiences and I realize how effective this can be. At least in my own work. And, uh, so when I can look at that and say, "Ok, we're going to be using a circle instead of a traditional classroom," immediately in my mind, I see a relaxed group of people sitting in a safe environment sharing. I think so many times the classroom experience is "I teach, you listen," whereas the Circle means that we all listen and share with one another.

And after three successful trips, we are aware that there is something unique about our relationships to each other, which may set the stage for positive Circles. It is not just the Circle structure; it is the way that the students perceive us. Our positive relationships with each other, and our positive past experiences with Circle, may have impacted our students in ways that we have never fully considered. This raises the question, "How important are perceived staff relationships when it comes to feelings of connection within the student body?" In small schools like ours, these staff relationships are significant models for healthy or unhealthy working relationships. Thus, while many programs focus on connectedness activities within the student body, administrators and program leaders may want to consider the implications of staff-staff relationships on student feelings of connectedness.

Circle Shifts Student Perceptions of Each Other

In addition to shifting student perceptions of teachers, Circle also served as a catalyst for perception changes within the peer group. A few students came into the trip carrying negative feelings towards one another that we as teachers did not know about at the time. Thus, the intention of our Talking Circles was not to repair harm, but it seemed to do so naturally in some cases.

In one case, specifically, this happened. Unknown to us, one of our students had been bullied by another during her younger years. Describing the event was clearly still painful.

> Student: The one student was the one that I've known for awhile. Um. He, uh, we used to live in the same area and I know like there were times where he would be one of the people to make fun of me (gently shook her head) and like, judge me because of my Dad's actions and not because of mine. But, after Circle, (slight smile) we became closer and found out the truth behind it, it was just really nice to feel a bit of closure in that.

> Amy: Do you feel that justice was kind of restored for you through Circle in that relationship? Like when you talk about closure…

> Student: Yeah. To know that they know that they did something wrong and to just come up to me and say "sorry" after the trip. So that was really nice.

The perpetrator of the past bullying also had similar feelings about the student above:

> Oh, yeah my impressions changed about her. I didn't like her when I was a little kid. She was a little tattletale. I'd known her since elementary school. But, yeah, she's nice. I learned that just because I didn't like her when I was a younger kid, I can't hold that against her—that's just how I felt when I was younger.

A different student recalled another previous conflict:

> There's one (student) from such a long time ago. I didn't expect to be going on the trip with him. When we were talking and stayed up one night after Circle, we just ended up talking about our differences from when we knew each other before until now. And we seemed to connect a little better.

Another student said of a still different conflict:

> I knew _____ from past experiences when we went to school. But from the past, I didn't like him at all. And then on the trip, we all ended up becoming friends.

When asked, "How did Circle ground that?" she said:

> Because Circle was where you could speak about anything. When you had the rock, or the object in your hand, no one else could speak and everyone paid attention to you. And, I don't know if it was a rule or anything, but I think it was just instinct for people to know not to go out and talk about people's issues behind their back or to anybody else. So that just opened up a big door for everyone. And everyone got to realize who they really are with Circle. Cuz we talked about the day, but then you could talk about anything else. And people would talk about their personal experiences, or what they'd be thinking about, or if something reminded them of something.

In each of these cases, a specific conflict-resolution Circle or peer-mediation Circle was not held. Instead, student perceptions about each other changed through the process of sharing personal stories. In many cases, schools tend to shift to results-oriented restorative practice. Schools wait for the tension to build and then work on mediation. Specific results are often hoped for or discussed. Circle, on the other hand, repaired relationships by giving students an opportunity to connect about things outside of the specific conflict. This idea of "detached reconnection" is interesting to me. Though many students clearly still thought about the previous conflict, they were detached from it. The Circle topics were about shared experiences rather than specific offenses. The results of this unsolicited reconnection and healing are significant. In an era of result-oriented strategies, are there possible forms of healing and repair that schools are failing to utilize?

In addition to speaking of repairing past relationships, students spoke openly about prejudging others and how Circle helped them work through that. Guy spoke openly about how Circle changed his perceptions of some of the girls:

> Because otherwise I couldn't see this person who dressed goth, if I was around her. Before I knew her...Before I got to hear what she had to say, I wouldn't have listened. I would have disagreed with whatever she's got to say. But once you sit down and listen, you realize that it don't matter who you are, everyone's got a heart. You all go through bad stuff and through good stuff. And there's a lot more that people go through than others do. And you just got to realize that everyone's different. And everyone's got something to say.

When I asked Guy what he learned from Circle, he once again brought up prejudging others:

> It's like to see what they've been through, and imagine yourself and what you'd been through, and you gotta welcome that person with open arms because if they're feeling like that and you've been in the same spot, you'd have wanted a hug too. I mean, just like that. That's mutual respect. That's what I've learned. Not to prejudge anyone. There was a lot of weird people for me to be on this trip with. I thought, "I'm never gonna talk to her" or say hello really. But then I ended up talking to the person every day, and joking about stuff, and just getting along. Everyone was getting along, so it was just great.

Adrienne spoke of prejudgment as well:

> I learned about what other people are going through. If I had any preconceived notions about that person before the trip, like in Circle, we got to

learn about what's going on in their lives. What they're feeling. Anything you had thought about them before—you kind of dropped that.

Faith spoke directly of prejudging based on clothing and style, something that she had felt a victim of in the past, as well as someone who held her own misconceptions of others:

> Once they go on that trip you realize that just because people dress in black clothes and wear heavy jeans and stuff, that doesn't mean that they're not people that want to go do fun and exciting things. You get to realize that just the way you dress...I can't say it...I don't know how. (Pause) Just because you wear baggy clothes and black jeans doesn't mean you're a bad person and that you don't want to do fun and exciting things that don't involve drugs and alcohol. You can't judge people on the way that they dress. Everyone has their own good qualities.

Sheila mentioned her preconceived notions of a boy on the trip:

> And then _____I saw a really different change in him too. When I first met him, I thought he was some country hick that didn't like black people or anything. Then we got into Circle and things were different.

The interviews shed light on relationships that left me wondering how Circle facilitated these changes. After analyzing the dialogue of the interviews, I noticed that three elements were mentioned repeatedly and seemed to lead to feelings of connectedness, belonging, and changes in perceptions of others. Those three elements are: relatedness, mutual respect/trust, and shared experience. In the next section, we will look closely at each element.

Shared Experience, Mutual Respect/Trust, and Relatedness

Another aspect of the trip that needs to be noted is that students were traveling away from the chaos of their own lives, and sharing an experience together. Many of the students interviewed had never been camping before and only one had been to South Dakota. Thus, some of the things that students mentioned about Circle were directly influenced by distance and close proximity to one another. A few students even noted that people opened up more in Circle the further away from home that they traveled. For example, Clyde said:

> Uh, well, when we first started, they weren't nearly as good as when we finished. No one opened up as much. Everyone started feeling a little bit safer the farther we got. We were so far away from home and it was basically all of us together so we had to trust one another a little bit more...We were all from the same area, the same school, we all had more trust with each other, than five different kids from five different teachers.

Distance must not have been the main factor, however, as it is interesting to note that we traveled back along the same route and most students listed the last Circle, the one when we were closest to home, as the most meaningful. Thus, I believe time together may have played a more important factor than distance.

It is important to mention that shared experience and Circle seemed to go hand in hand with each other in student responses. There were more factors at work than just Circle. Sheila mentioned this notion of connectedness as a result of the combination of shared experience and Circle:

> You can like, meet someone and think something of them, but when you sit them down and their actual feelings about things you've experienced together come out, you, like, have to be close to that person because you know what they're talking about. You experienced it too. It's a really good way to open yourself up and like learn more about people too and yourself.

Clyde spoke of the shared experience being an effective topic during Circle, something that separated previous types of Circles in his mind:

> Clyde: The only Circles I'd been around before the trip were peer mediation or a Circle about what I'd done over the weekend, nothing about how I feel or nothing the way it was on the trip.
>
> Amy: So tell me about how was it different on the trip?
>
> Clyde: The way we talked. The way we shared our experiences. The way we looked at things differently and how we all felt about it as we saw it.

When asked what we did in Circle and what she learned from Circle, Adrienne responded:

> We shared our experiences and we learned about different things... I learned the importance of togetherness. I think that's an obvious one. Cuz we weren't just going on a trip. We were going together. I think that was probably one of the most important things on the trip. Just being together.

Randy Bauer recalled memories from our 2004 trip in which shared experience brought Hmong and Native American males together. He recalled:

> After Circles, they were talking more to each other. They were more at ease with each other. They weren't posturing through talk or B.S. These kids are forced to be together and that's a facilitator itself. One of the things that facilitated it, when you have two very diverse groups experiencing the same thing and doing what all human beings do, laughing together, slapping their sides together, crying together, eating together, working together—they are together. The other stuff just falls apart. They would have never gotten together here at school. But they shared a common positive experience. A common positive experience of sharing. Circle helped them reflect on that.

Guy showed the importance of shared experience when he thought of the current relationships of the students. The trip is over, but that shared experience has not been forgotten. But again, he does not seem to separate Circle from that shared experience. He said:

> I know that whenever we see each other, I mean when we look at each other we know that we've been places before, like on an adventure. And it was fun. When I see everyone that we had in our Circle, we just know. I know that I've heard what they've had to say about things and I know who they are. It helps me to just be able to say hi.

The adventure of the journey may have impacted the students as well. Guy said:

> The one Circle that I do remember was when everyone was leaving. It was our last Circle and I looked in everyone's eyes and I knew everyone wanted to go back to our regular life. But I knew a part of them wanted to say, "Let's just hit the road and keep on going. And go farther and farther." Because we

could have. (Pause. Smile) No, but...I just know just by looking at everyone that they knew that this doesn't happen a lot...and that they were going to miss it.

In addition to a shared experience, the development of mutual respect and trust was linked to positive feelings of Circle. Guy mentioned trust when speaking of things that he learned in Circle:

> Well, because hearing them talk, everyone has a chance to talk and you've got to listen. I don't know, you get the same respect as everyone else when you're talking.

Mary addressed group respect in her interview:

> I believe Circle impacted us a lot because everyone who went cared about their feelings and the feelings of others and what they had to say or what they believed, whether it was different from someone else or the same. Everyone let others opinions be opinions and not just something to fight about because of what others' beliefs are! Everyone was able to see that, so I think it had a big impact on everyone because what they said was respected!

This notion of respect was tied to being able to share feelings without facing judgment from teachers or students. Somehow, as Mary said, conflicting beliefs and experiences were respected by all members of the Circle. During all three trips, there was never a time when someone interrupted another person, spoke only to disagree or agree with another person, or expressed negativity about another person's feelings. This is remarkable. Part of this was due to the structure of Circle and the honoring of the talking piece. The ritual seemed to elicit respect because the rules and codes were clear to everyone. In many schools today, the rules and codes do not hold meaning for students, or the rules and codes seem to shift. In the case of Circle, students understood that respect meant listening openly and setting judgment aside. They understood that the rule to speak only when holding the talking piece worked because they felt validated by having active listeners when it was their turn. For teachers, this lesson is extremely important, as we often interject when our students begin speaking in our classrooms. Or we try to verbally guide students to an answer that seems appropriate. We rarely follow the rules of Circle and listen attentively and respectfully to students speak until they are ready to stop. To students, this uninterrupted talking time equaled respect. This definition of respect helped me become a more attentive listener in my classroom, but I still have a long way to go.

Though mutual respect and trust are mentioned, they are often layered within reflections on relating to others. Though no interview question directly asked about relatedness, each and every student mentioned it.

For Faith, trust and relatedness go hand in hand. Prior to the trip, she was generally a student who had trouble trusting others and often would walk around the school in complete silence. When asked what made her comfortable in Circle, she said:

> The people. And I don't know. If you expressed how you felt they wouldn't say anything to make fun of you or say anything mean. There was a lot of people that could relate to the stuff that you'd be talking about, so, that helped also.

Hannah directly speaks of both connectedness and relating to others. She said:

> Circle gives you a connection. When you…when you hear things about how other people are you're kind of like, "Oh you're like me." When you put walls — you don't have so many walls up when you first meet people. I don't think it would have the same effect. You learn little details that you have in common. When you have things in common, you tend to be able to connect to people better.

I recorded an experience of relatedness in my 2004 journal:

> It's amazing to see the Hmong students and Native American students finding a shared history. As we read about the loss of Lakota land before Circle, ____ and ____ began speaking of their land in Laos as being stripped away. They shared stories of grandparents on reservations and in Thai refugee camps. I never expected that. I don't know why, but I didn't even think of that. To see these kids, so very different, not knowing each other at all before the trip, talking and sharing stories was amazing. They related to each other through their own histories. Soon, ____ began asking how to say Hmong words and language lessons were being shared.

Clyde believed Circle served as a catalyst for further connection outside of Circle. He said:

> Yeah. There. Yeah...It [Circle] changed us a lot. Even when us students weren't around the teachers we'd talk about problems we had at home and how we related to them.

Sometimes the ability to relate to one another brought about a complex range of emotions. During many evening Circles, students and teachers cried. Sheila spoke specifically about relatedness when asked about why people cried when in Circle:

> Well, I don't know, I think it's because you don't realize your emotions sometimes until you like force them to come out. And Circle is a good way to do that, because people talk and you listen... You kind of listen to people and sometimes you relate it to yourself. And sometimes you feel bad if someone is expressing their pain or something. You just see that person on a different level and it just brings out a lot of emotions.

Faith also brought up emotions shown in Circle and her feelings of relatedness due to problems the students have faced. She said:

> I think that Circle was really like, emotional because a lot of people let out feelings that they won't tell anyone and probably haven't written down. I think it was a really good thing cuz it let people see that just cuz they have lots of problems in life, you don't have to base life on problems. That you have to enjoy the good times you have with the people around you.

Relatedness seemed to impact many of the students in positive ways and may have fostered transformative learning. Though the students were all extremely diverse, they found commonality. Taylor (2009) writes "social interaction and dialogue have been found to lead to consensual validation (valid by the process of discussing it) among learners" (p. 9). Baumgartner's (2002) research on transformational learning showed that patients who were diagnosed HIV-positive found community and felt less alone. In regard to our students, it was not just because of having lived through similar situations; it was about experiencing similar feelings too. When one student shared an emotion, other students were able to recall times that they felt similar pain, wonder, or joy. I think that many teachers believe that student situations must be the same in order to foster relatedness; but, in fact, students spoke of relating to the emotions that someone shared. The circumstances in their lives did not need to relate; rather it was the emotions that they shared that often drew students together.

Connectedness

Along with sharing an experience, speaking in a trusting environment, and relating to one another, students spoke openly about connectedness. This was perhaps the most obvious transformative response that we, as teachers, saw. We saw connection grow out of the safety of the Circles that we established. I wrote in a June, 2006 journal:

> It's amazing to see _____ open up like this. I don't think I remember seeing her smile all year. I was worried about her opening up and she completely astonished me. Circle seems to weave a feeling of connection through her whole being. She talks, she listens...she glows. She has been transformed.

This connection with peers and staff transferred to a connection with the curriculum. I continue reflecting about the same student:

> I've never seen her so connected to learning either. On our walk in the foothills, she searched for bones and flowers. She came upon a whole set of bones and proudly showed everyone. She then began using scientific method to figure out where the bones came from.

Randy Bauer also spoke of student transformation when I asked him about memories that stood out for him:

> One of the things that I found which absolutely flabbergasted me with these kids is that I saw their defenses go down in these Circles. When people are vulnerable and they don't let anybody in. When you feel vulnerable and you have been hurt, you keep any of your feelings in a lock box, with battle plate armor, 400 thousand chains and paddle locks and no one is gonna get in there. No one. Because the horrendous fear is getting hurt again. And the feeling is, "I've been hurt once and dammit, no one is ever going to hurt me again..." In the Circle, I found, and I, I, thought I'd never see this happen, and I saw it on both field trips, I saw these kids' defenses come down and

they cried. Some of them cried and some of them were so honest. And I said, "You are so wonderful for sharing this. You would never....this would be something that never would have been said in a thousand years in the regular classroom because you don't have permission... you're too...you can't do it. You're too vulnerable. You're too vulnerable to be hurt."

These kids felt safe enough to risk and with that risk there's possibility for tremendous growth. Because growth sometimes requires pain, it requires risk, and we provided that opportunity through the Circle. This is the pathway. There are probably lots of other paths, but this is the one that we found works quite well with these kids. And I found that...I found that just amazing.

As teachers with many years of experience working with alternative youth, Angel, Randy, and I have seen students begin our trips with complete feelings of disconnection. Many of the students on our past trips have exhibited feelings of disconnection in a variety of ways. Some students had confrontations with other staff and other students, some were withdrawn and spoke only to one or two teachers, some wore layers of clothes hoping to hide beneath them, most were a year behind academically, while others harmed themselves through cutting or drug abuse. The fact that our students reported feelings of connectedness is amazing.

Hannah spoke of her feelings of connectedness in the following conversation during our interview:

Hannah: I learned that I could connect with people so easy. That I could make friends so easy. I've never made friends easy.

Amy: How did that connection make you feel?

Hannah: Moved. I don't know any other way to put it.

Suzy spoke of her feelings of connectedness in terms of community. She said the following about Circle:

It impacted us by bringing us together. And just getting to know each other a little more or something you didn't know about that person or what was truly troubling them inside. And our community just got really, we were, we all revolved around each other. So, it was like bringing everybody together.

She later recalled our first Circle:

> Probably after the first night after getting to our first campground site was the one that stuck out the most because we got to know each other a little bit and we got to know the feel of how it is going to be every night and just being able to hear everybody's opinion about that day and how different it was from life at home. And basically hearing everybody's feelings and starting to get to know each other, like pulling everybody together. It was really neat to see how that process just pulled everybody together.

Other students spoke of connectedness using the language of friendship. Jackie said, "I found out about everybody's life. And we all became close friends."

Adrienne also spoke of friendships. She also introduced the concept of Circle fostering feelings of "family":

> Well, like I said, we just got closer. They weren't just my teachers and some kids, we were all like, friends, and practically a little family. Just going through all that together brought us so much closer than when we started out.

Jackie directly described the group using the term family. She said:

> It felt like I had another family. I felt like...people really cared about me, because you got to speak about what we did throughout the day and we always had fun...And at the end of the day, you got to talk about that. And people stopped and listened to you and looked at you in your eyes when you were talking. And, it just made you feel like you were loved. And I know there are some people in there who probably feel distant from their families and don't feel loved, and I'm pretty sure, pretty positive, that they got that feeling that you know, they were loved by them. They might not say it, or admit it to this day, but you can see it in people's eyes and how they act that that was another family in Circle. (Smiles)

Clyde, who also gave me permission to use his journal entries, wrote this about Circle:

> Circle was great. I think it brought everyone much closer. I don't know how to describe our last Circle. It made me feel incredible. Some of my favorite campfire Circles were when everyone said how they felt more comfortable

and how they felt we were like a family. It feels good to have people, actually strangers, say that about you.

An additional way that students spoke of connectedness was by speaking of belonging. Suzy said of her peers in Circle:

> They just asked for my true feelings on things. And I actually felt like I got to speak for myself and not pretend I was somebody else. And…it just made me feel that I was part of something. It just brought me closer to everybody. And it felt really good to be a part of something.

Guy also spoke of belonging:

> There were a lot of Circles and every time I felt closer to someone. By the end of the trip, I felt safe, so, like, I belonged.

With each and every interview, I asked if students missed Circle and every one of them said "yes." Many had tears well in their eyes. Many said, "I'd do it all over again in a heartbeat."

When asked why she misses Circle, Adrienne said:

> The people. And…you don't really get that every day. That chance to connect with everybody. You just kind of go about your daily lives. We had a moment to just slow down. But, everybody's so busy, normally we don't connect like that. [Pause] Yeah. [Looks at the camera and smiles.]

Angel Salathe speaks of this connectedness in terms of community. She also believes that the concept of community helps prevent conflict:

> I truly believe that the Circle process both builds and strengthens community. The peer community that the Circle is made of, usually enables participants the space to work through issues that may arise or have arisen. For instance, when taking students on week-to-ten-day westward expeditions, camping and being with one another twenty-four/seven, people tend to get on one another's nerves. We tend to have participants lose their patience with each other. When this happens morning and evening Circle time gives us the opportunity to work through these issues together as a community. The clear and open, positive space that the Circle gives, enables us to have conversations we normally would not be able to have.

Randy Bauer also speaks of community. He said, of working with youth labeled at-risk:

> In our tiny, tiny way, Circle is promoting community. And then the sky is the limit. This is what we are doing. This is the greatest gift you can give these kids is a sense of community.

According to students, part of this concept of connectedness and community was a result of revelations shared in Circle. Many students shared the metaphor of removing masks. When asked what she learned through Circle, Suzy said:

> About myself I learned that I don't have to put a mask on every day that I should be proud of who I am. Not my actions or what I look like or what everybody judges about me. And uh, to learn that everybody underneath the mask... they are a different person and that so many people put on a mask. It's just really weird how many people are in my position and feel the same thing that I feel. Just that no matter how tough somebody is that they have a problem too. And just to be able to admit to their problems is really amazing and to hear about it and stuff.

When I asked Suzy if people just put the mask back on after Circle, she replied:

> I think after it, I think they reflect on it a little while before they put their mask on. I mean, it doesn't take it off permanently, but it could take it off for a point in time. And after replaying what you said in Circle, it just makes you reflect on, "Hey, I really don't need it. And that I shouldn't be afraid of showing everybody who I really am." I think it sticks with somebody for a long time before they decide to put it back on.

Faith also spoke of masks:

> Circle is a way to uncover all the masks and cover ups that people put on for school and for social events. Circle is just a way that you can see the inner self of everyone and see the true beauty that lies behind people.

Jackie did not use the metaphor of masks, but said that Circle helped her see true personalities. She combined this knowledge with pre-judgments as well:

I was kind of intrigued to find out everyone else's personality. They didn't...the way they looked didn't fit their personality. They really had a sweet personality... I look at people in a different perspective, not because of what they wear or their race, but I try to find out their personality. And listen to them.

Guy spoke of sharing of himself and simply said, "I'm glad that I showed myself to everyone."

As teachers we recognize this ability to reveal honest character as one important result of safe Circles. In my interview with Randy Bauer, he spoke directly of this being one of the greatest benefits of Circle:

I think one of the great benefits of Circle is that for the first time these kids have been honest with themselves. How cool is that? For maybe the first time, these kids have been honest with themselves and faced themselves. And that's a big step. And it's like the poem about the man in the mirror. You see? Who is that? And that's you. Well, is that what you perceive? And for the first time, they've seen a reflection. A reflection of themselves and who they really are. And this is why some of them realize for the first time that they're seeing themselves without distortion and they really are... "For the first time I've seen who I really am and it's not as bad as I thought it was! It's OK to be who I am. And I don't have to be this other thing—what I pretended I was. It's OK to be who I am this way." And that is tremendously releasing. And once you've let go of the thing you pretended to be, then there's all this energy to grow what you can be. The Circle is a springboard for that...And as for relationships with each other, Circle allows a method of clearing the waters and the fog to see what the other person is really like in a safe way.

All of these concepts seemed to mix together to form feelings of connectedness. When students felt safe to share their own personalities, they realized that they all had a great deal in common. This relatedness and shared experience led to feelings of family and belonging. It is very difficult to separate any of these ideas of connectedness because they all rolled together. Students would speak of one concept and layer the other in the same sentence.

Additional Results of Circle Experience

Along with promoting feelings of connectedness, it is important to note that students brought up other results of time spent in Circle. Something that many students spoke of was that Circle gave them time to reflect on what they saw, what they learned through mini-lessons, and what they felt about their experiences.

Adrienne spoke of reflection and connection as a result of Circle:

> Adrienne: I think it [Circle] was pretty important. We needed that after a long day and everything that happened. Just to reflect on everything. It made a pretty big impact.
>
> Amy: How did it help you reflect on the day?
>
> Adrienne: We'd all share our experiences of what went on. But, we just had our individual experiences. And once we were in Circle, it kind of became one.

Jackie also spoke of reflection and a motivation to capture reflections in writing:

> And Circle time was just so much fun to go and reflect. And everyone at the end would go and write in their journal and everyone actually did it. They didn't have a problem doing it. A lot of kids would, I guess. So I remember that.

Both teachers spoke of Circle as a tool for reflection and assessment as well. Angel Salathe said:

> I do think that Circle is an effective reflection tool for evaluating student learning. During our expeditions, it was by far the best and easiest way to know how much our students were taking in, learning, and retaining...I believe Circles allow students an atmosphere to communicate what they have experienced or learned and link it to the background knowledge they already possess. I have seen students who were not able to express themselves or what they learned by taking a "traditional" test or assessment, able to articulate their new experiences and knowledge in a manner not familiar to them. Circle brings about a sort of serendipitous climate that breeds success for students and opens a possibility for conveying their new acquired wisdom.

Randy Bauer also spoke of Circle as a way to promote reflection and to assess understanding:

> In Circle and through interaction with you, I can probably get a better understanding if "Yeah, you get it. You get what I'm trying to say to you." And I think that a Circle has the ability to better facilitate that. There's many ways of doing it, you can do it in the classroom, with the tests and everything, but the Circle is one way of doing that. On our field trips , sitting around the campfire, there is closure for the day. Ok. And if I'm interacting with the group. Some of the open ended questions, "What did you learn today?"

When asked about this method, Randy described reflection in Circle compared to other forms of assessment:

> Circle is the processing piece. With Circle, you put it on the hard drive. It's locked in. And then from there you can further process. You've got these experiences, you've got Circle, you've got journals, and then you have the life processing piece. I think we call the test the processing piece here (at school), but with our Circle, we are dealing with a holistic approach… With Circle gone, you won't address the whole person.

In addition to Circle promoting reflection, students, such as Adrienne, spoke of Circle promoting feelings of peace and calm:

> Circle was really calming. And just the whole, being at night and sitting there all together. It brought the day to a close really well.

Suzy described her Circle experiences as putting her in a "peace zone." Faith also said, "It was a good thing to do. It was a good stress reliever."

In addition to feelings of peace and calm, students reported feeling more positive about life. Faith speaks of her time in Circle and her time on the trip as being transformative:

> I know that I've changed a lot. Before I went on it, I didn't want to go on this trip. I really didn't want to. But, I'm really glad I did because you got to know people, and you got to do fun and exciting things outside. And things that are actually healthy for you…Now the way I look at it is that you can't just walk around being mad all the time, just being angry. There is really good things out there. You gotta make the best out of life.

Clyde spoke of how Circle impacted him:

> I didn't remember, really think about anything from before [the trip]. I just kept thinking positive about the future. I didn't relate on anything that I didn't want to relate on anymore. Things that brought me down I didn't want to think about them no more just because I was so happy being around the people I was with. Being able to share the feelings that I had.

Hannah also spoke of Circle leading to positive thoughts:

> No matter what you've been put through there's more to life than what you see. You can always get out of the bad things and have hope that it'll get better.

Not only did Circle create positive feelings while on the trip, time spent in Circle created positive feelings about people in general. Sheila's interview was eight months after the trip and she said:

> I learned from Circle that alternative kids aren't bad. So that was really cool. [speaking quickly, merging into the next sentence] I learned from myself umm, that like, there's not really a point in like shutting oneself out, because there's always someone who can help you. There's always someone who can inspire you or make you feel better or can relate to something that's happened to you. Even if you're like, "This is the worst thing ever! I'm the only person who knows what's going on." Someone can make you feel better. So I really think that's a good thing to learn. So whatever. [Smiles and laughs.]

Healing and Circle

In addition to thoughts of peace and calm, students also described the healing experience of Circle. Though I did not ask about healing directly, students spoke of it, especially in regard to the ritual of our last Circle. This was the ritual described in the introduction. Students were invited to journal about things that they would like to "leave in the mountains." Almost every student mentioned this initial step to our last Circle. Even though a physical fire did not exist due to being stormed out, students recall "burning" their papers, even though they actually folded them beneath the lamp to be burned later by Mr. Bauer. When asked what he learned from Circle, Clyde described that night:

It's changed. There are things that when they get brought up now, I just push them aside and I think about that last night in Circle, when I burnt that piece of paper.

Clyde's awareness that he responded differently to things after the trip showed evidence of transformative learning. When confronted with old patterns of responding to anger, he was able to reflect back on Circle, regroup and respond in a different way.

When asked to share a specific memory of Circle, Guy also recalled that night, but does not remember the specifics about the pieces of paper:

We were in the hotel room. That Circle was really...that one affected me. It made me cry because you guys talked about regrets that we had in the past and that we were all going to write it and put it in a jar. And I remember...I just knew everyone was emptying out what they had to say. I know I did. By the time I was done with it I was crying. I don't know. It felt good to rip that up. That's what I remember most. Us in the room. The pink hoody over the lamp that made it look like the fire. The dim lighting. It was great.

Only one student specifically used the word healing, but she rejected that term. Faith said of her most memorable Circle:

Well, probably one of them would be the one that I was talking about before when we all wrote something down on paper. I didn't feel healed, but I felt relief. Like... like, I felt like I could breathe again and not constantly be thinking about all the bad stuff. It helped me release the bad stuff and just think about the good stuff in life.

These notions of healing, though difficult to describe, happened on all of our trips. Each teacher has memories of specific students that seemed deeply moved because of Circle. When I asked Randy Bauer if Circle promoted healing, he responded:

Oh certainly. Anytime, anytime a human being risks and is acknowledged and validated. Do you think these kids have been validated in their lives? Very few of them. That promotes healing. "It's OK that that happened to you. It's OK." Any human being, we hold on to so much baggage and that encumbers us, and in a Circle, if you say something and you realize that it's OK, you are validated. And you let go. And when you let go a healing process occurs. When you let go of negative thoughts or hatred, jealousy, that are counterproductive...in Circle there is the chance to divulge and to risk and to let go. Once you are validated you can let go, and heal, and move on.

Though the transformative aspects of healing are difficult to define, we witnessed the process of letting go of old hurts in a safe environment. Each student returned from these trips with the same problems, but most now do not recall the specific things that they wrote about in their paper. Or, as Clyde said, they now handle their problems in a different way. Realistically, I acknowledge that Circle is not a magic solution and that it does not heal all wounds. Unfortunately, we were made very aware of that when one of our students died of a drug overdose in 2006. Painfully aware of the limitations of Circle, Angel and I attended his funeral and grieved deeply over that loss. As Faith says, perhaps Circle creates breathing space for troubled youth, and validates the feeling in that moment, but there are limitations to what Circle can heal. Our Circles, especially, were not meant to be Healing Circles, but it is still important to note that moments of healing and release were described by many of the students.

Margaret also described Circle as a "spiritual place." O'Sullivan's (2002) vision statement on transformative learning states:

> I believe that any in-depth treatment of transformative education must address the topic of spirituality and that educators must take on the development of the spirit at a most fundamental level. Contemporary education today suffers deeply by its eclipse of the spiritual dimension of our world and universe. (p. 10)

Through the rituals of smudging sage, lighting a fire, reflecting, and sharing a space in Circle, we were able to bring aspects of spirituality into education. Even though only one student described Circle as a spiritual place, Angel, Randy and I have often used the term "spiritual" to describe our time spent in Circle.

Throughout the interviews, it was very clear that students had positive feelings about the evening Circles that they experienced. Students reported that Circle helped change their perspectives of staff and of peers. Students also felt that they related to others through

Circle, that they felt connected to each other, and that Circle helped them remove some of their masks. In addition, students reported feelings of peace and some evidence of a healing process. Students changed as a result of Circle and left feeling more positive. They believed that Circle was a positive means of reflection.

In summary, Circle served to foster feelings of connectedness. It provided a safe place for students to voice their real thoughts and opinions. It allowed them to process and reflect on a day filled with curriculum. It created feelings of community. This method of creating a place for dialogue and for establishing relationships with our students did foster transformative learning. Students began to change their thoughts about stereotypes, felt healing, and returned home handling their problems in a "different way." Our next chapter explores the question, "Do restorative justice Circles restore justice?" Chapter Four details our belief that restorative justice Circles cannot exist in isolation in school programs. Instead, the use of Circle needs to be combined with social justice and human rights education that further fosters transformative learning.

Multicultural Education, Human Rights Education, and Teaching for Social Justice: Transforming Ideas about History, Racial Identity, and Service

Multicultural education theory, human rights education, and an emphasis on teaching for social justice are all essential elements of our program's approach towards educational pedagogy and curriculum development. Three questions have guided the research in this chapter:

- Did any students undergo transformational learning as a result of using a multicultural and social justice approach when teaching Westward Expansion curriculum?
- What impact did human rights education have on student learning?
- What did our students learn about social justice? Did the use of restorative justice Talking Circles "restore justice" for any participants?

In order to begin discussing these topics, it is essential to look at who Randy, Angel, and I are as educators and what brought us to this work and what enabled us to become multicultural. How did our own practice and beliefs concerning social justice and multicultural education frame the curriculum that we developed? Being multicultural is defined as a process whereby an individual develops competencies of perceiving, evaluating, believing, and doing in multiple ways (Banks, 1988). Research shows that teachers who come from bicultural backgrounds have a greater understanding of social injustice, which better prepares them to teach social justice curriculum (Park, 2008, p. 205). Though all three of us are White, each of us was exposed to human rights and social justice through a wide variety of life experiences and education. Randy had bicultural experiences living and working for years on a reservation in Minnesota, and through his teaching in Costa Rica. In addition, he was an active advocate for environmental justice and attended classes on social justice. Angel has the unique experience of being a lesbian educator, and has faced injustices in the educational system herself as a result. She also has years of experience teaching in urban settings and being involved in both the Native American and Hispanic communities where she has taught.

I became interested in issues of diversity at a young age. I grew up reading literature from around the world and my parents say that I was always concerned about injustice in the world. College classes exposed me to a wider variety of literature by diverse authors. However, it was when I became a teacher that I became solidly grounded in multicultural education because of my experiences with my students. During my first years of teaching, I began reading and listening to the stories of my students' lives. As an English teacher at an alternative school, I had the great gift of smaller class sizes, and flexible scheduling. I had the time to really develop relationships with my students, and it was through their writing, projects, and class discussions that I began to learn about the diverse voices within our community. Like Julie Landsman in *A White Teacher Talks About Race* (2001), I learned a great deal from my alternative school students regarding race and culture because we had close relationships and my students allowed me to make mistakes, explained their points of view, and shared their life stories. Landsman's book inspired me to explore my own successes and recognize my inadequacies. Because of this self-reflection, I began taking classes on educational equity, multicultural education, and human rights education and incorporated those lessons into my teaching. For two years, I attended Seeking Educational Equity and Diversity (SEED) courses on inclusive curriculum, which is a program founded by Peggy McIntosh. The program calls on participants to investigate elements of critical race theory, such as white privilege (McIntosh, 1988), and to challenge his or her thinking about equity, diversity, and social justice. Critical Race Theory in education, as argued by Ladson-Billings and Tate (1995), stresses the importance of three perspectives when studying inequities in education: race continues to be significant in the United States; U.S. society is based on property rights rather than human rights; and the intersections of race and property create an analytical tool for understanding inequity.

Though far from an expert on this topic, I embraced the ideas because I began to see the truth of them within the walls of my alternative school. Why was there a disproportionate amount of low-income, homeless students being referred to the alternative school as truants or failing students? Why were there a disproportionate number of students of color being referred to our alternative school? The two years of SEED courses served as transformational learning experiences for me and encouraged me to develop strategies for breaking down inequalities in the school districts and communities where I taught. Prior to SEED, I was a quiet advocate because I felt like, "Hey, I'm just a White girl from the prairie, I shouldn't be talking about race. Only people of color have that right." Thus, the most transformational element of the program was the confidence that I gained and the belief that White teachers must be actively involved in social justice and policy change regarding equity in education. In my classroom, I began incorporating readings into the curriculum that showed multiple perspectives. According to Adams (1997):

> In addition to offering a focused analysis of systemic racism, critical race theory (CRT) offers educators an innovative approach to "voice" by posing argument through the use of metaphorical tales, chronicles, and "counternarratives" synthesized from multiple historical, sociological, and personal, anecdotal, familial sources. (p. 25)

Using *Counternarratives* (Solórzano and Yosso, 2002), a tool to counter deficit-informed research and stories about people of color, I began providing stories and nonfiction articles by people of color that countered mainstream stereotypes, such as the poetry of Luis Rodríguez (2005) and Sherman Alexie (1992). I found that my students loved the stories and that reading the stories helped students begin to write and speak about their own families, culture, and values. I also began using student stories and voices in qualitative research. I began

interviewing students about dropout prevention, alternative education, and the types of classrooms that they wanted. Though informal,
these first interviews enabled me to formulate new ideas concerning
programming such as developing multicultural clubs and mentorship
programs.

In addition to these individual experiences, Randy, Angel, and I
all had collective experiences regarding alternative students. Being at
an alternative school, a place often thought of as a "dumping ground"
for underperforming students and a building that held a disproportionate number of students of color, we all saw the educational inequities in our school system. We saw that a higher number of students
of color faced suspensions and expulsions in our district. We listened
as our students told us of the injustices in their earlier classrooms and
their feelings that they were judged because they learned differently
or "weren't the perfect student." The summer school program that we
created was one way to fight the injustices because it presented a new
way of teaching and learning for our students. Though each of our
journeys to becoming multicultural educators is varied and complex,
we share common beliefs about the importance of including multicultural education and a human rights framework in our curriculum and
teaching pedagogies.

Banks and Banks (1995) write the following description of multicultural education:

> Multicultural education is field of study and an emerging discipline whose
> major aim is to create equal educational opportunities for students from di-
> verse racial, ethnic, social-class, and cultural groups. One of its important
> goals is to help all students to acquire the knowledge, attitudes, and skills
> needed to function effectively in a pluralistic democratic society and to in-
> teract, negotiate, and communicate with peoples from diverse groups in or-
> der to create a civic and moral community that works for the common good.
> (p. xi)

Gomez (1991) states that multicultural education "embodies a perspective rather than a curriculum" (¶ 11). He further explains that
teachers must learn about their students, consider their students' cultural identities, be aware of their own biases, and learn and teach

about oppression. Banks (1997) states that multicultural education is an idea, an educational movement, and a process. It is important to note that I will use the phrase "curriculum" in this chapter, yet I recognize that multicultural education embodies complex ideas and is much more than texts, resources, or lesson plans. Because of this, I will also attempt to describe our ideas, approaches, and discussions regarding multicultural education.

Before delving into the research questions, it is important for the reader to have an understanding about elements of the Westward Bound curriculum. The first aspect of our curriculum, multicultural education, is best explored through Banks's (2004) five core dimensions of multicultural education. I will briefly describe each core dimension and will then detail how our Westward Bound program aligned with each core and how our students responded.

Content Integration

The first dimension is content integration—infusing the curriculum with material from diverse groups (Banks, 2004). When Angel and I began developing the history and English curriculum, we knew that we wanted to retell the story of Westward Expansion through the eyes of the many people involved in the story—not just through the recollections of male-dominated history texts. Though we did use texts by non-Indian authors, such as D. Brown's (1998) *Bury My Heart At Wounded Knee*, we also provided poetry, history, and storytelling from Native American authors. Students read excerpts from *The Journey of Crazy Horse* by J. Marshall III (2004), as well as J. Marshall's 2002 book, *The Lakota Way: Stories and Lessons for Living*. I shared poetry by Sherman Alexie (1992), Louise Erdrich (2003), Joy Harjo (2004), and N. Scott Momaday (2000). In addition, I packed anthologies of Native American poetry that students could read throughout the trip. We also were sure to include opportunities for students to read traditional stories and included books by Hazen-Hammond (1999) on Native American tales about women, and the book *Santee Dakota Indian Legends* edited by Woolworth (2003). Through all of this reading, we reminded students of the many diverse tribes within the United

States and that our trip only covered one aspect of the removal of people from their native land. As Kumashiro (2001) argues, knowledge from any text, such as pioneer women's letters, or Native American stories, would be partial:

> Such partiality means that, inevitably, the text will reflect the realities of some people but miss those of others; it will represent the voices of some groups but silence those of others; and in doing so, it will challenge some stereotypes while reinforcing others. (p. 7)

Discussing the complexity of this with students enabled them to see themes and connections while still understanding that there is no "one truth."

One of the themes that students connected to was that of forced removal from one's land. This theme introduced other diverse literature into our curriculum. In addition to Ojibwe students, Hmong and African American students also participated in our program. As we dove deeper into the history of forced removal in the West, Hmong students began sharing their family histories of forced removal from Laos. When learning about boarding schools that forced Native American youth to stop speaking English, Hmong students began sharing their stories about the difficulties of being "forced" to participate in the new American culture and their recollections of life in a refugee camp. Thus, I included poetry and short story readings from Moua's Hmong anthology *Bamboo Among the Oaks* (2002). When speaking of Native American boarding school students who were forcibly "renamed," students made the connection to Africans who were kidnapped and forced into slavery and also "renamed." Thus, poetry by African American poets such as Alice Walker (2003) and Langston Hughes (1990) were included in our readings. We agree with researchers who write that another element of content integration is allowing students the freedom to incorporate stories and themes that reflect who they are and what they want to investigate (Collatos and Morrell, 2003; Zirkel, 2008). By studying the literature within the curriculum and then sharing stories of their own family histories, students began seeing global connections around the theme of forced removal. Helping students make connections between their communities and national and global identities is one aspect of Ladson-Billings' culturally relevant practices that improve the educational experiences of students of color (Ladson-Billings, 1994).

Additionally, we also included women's voices in our curriculum. Students heard excerpts from the journals of pioneer women in such texts by O'Brien (1999), Holmes (1995), and Luchetti (2001). These real letters and diaries dismantled many stereotypes about women on the frontier, including stereotypes of the woman's role only being that of mother and cook. In some cases, women lost their husbands on the journey West and became the head of their own households or business leaders in their new communities. One student asked, "Why aren't these letters shown in mainstream schools?" Our student's awareness that something was missing from the traditional curriculum enabled students to start vocalizing growing beliefs that these missing voices were a sign of unequal representation.

Knowledge Construction — Transformational Learning via Wounded Knee

Banks's second dimension concerns knowledge construction—an awareness of and focus on the way that cultural frames shape the identification and interpretation of educational content (Banks, 2004, pp. 20–21). Our use of certain texts in our curriculum reinforced the idea that cultural frames shape the interpretation of historical events. For example, our curriculum discussed the diverse perspectives of the term "Westward Expansion." Students read newspaper articles from the time and saw the glorification of heading West and the way that Native Americans were portrayed through the media. It was evident during class discussions that students clearly determined that what was considered a positive event for one group could be a negative for another. We also showed the complexity of cultural framing by sharing stories about African American settlers and Chinese rail workers. One student wrote about this complexity in her journal:

> Uuugh! I don't know why Whites couldn't see all the groups that they were hurting. Why they didn't listen to all of the people involved. They were just

focused on gold, railroads, and themselves. The pain that other groups were feeling wasn't even something that was looked at.

Students displayed their knowledge about cultural framing in other ways as well. For example, during the trip, students began actively looking for all perspectives when we stopped at museums. If someone's "side" wasn't present, students began asking museum guides questions such as, "So, how did the museum get these items? Did you get permission from the tribe?" or "You only have two stories about women, why don't you have more?" These questions demonstrated knowledge of cultural framing; students were digging deeper and asking quality questions.

Another example was reading about the Battle of Wounded Knee from military records and notes versus the stories recorded by the victims of the massacre. Students saw that even though both parties were physically present at the event, the eyewitness testimonies were completely different based on which "side" of the issue they were on or to which culture the eyewitness identified.

For many students, experiencing the Wounded Knee Museum was one of the most powerful, transformational pieces of the program. Prior to the trip, most of our students could not describe the story of Wounded Knee. As teachers, we discussed and reflected on the possible student responses to the visit. We recognized the sensitive subject matter, and carefully planned our day with the museum first, followed by lunch and reflection time, then the wildlife loop in Custer State Park, and then evening Circle. Though always cautious in our planning for the day, we believed the museum was an important part of our curriculum. However, the visit did bring about feelings of anger, shame, and sadness for students. Mezirow refers to an experience like this as a "disorienting dilemma" (Mezirow, 1991). He states, "Transformational learning, especially when it involves subjective reframing, is often an intensely threatening emotional experience in which we have to become aware of both the assumptions undergirding our ideas and those supporting our emotional responses to the need to change" (Mezirow, 2000, p. 7). Other multicultural researchers describe moments like learning the facts about Wounded

Knee by using the psychological term of "cognitive dissonance"--a feeling of imbalance in which people accept a new idea or framework or employ "intellectual armor" and refuse to consider new possibilities (Gorski, 2009). Brookfield (1990) refers to transformative learning triggered by the awareness that what was once thought permanent and stable was suddenly observed to be relative and situation-specific. For our students, learning about what their government did to innocent women and children propelled them to look deeply at their ideas of government, race, and social justice and transformed their "blind trust" (as one student called it) of previous notions of history and government.

Before entering the museum, we let students know that some of the stories might cause distress and that we were there to listen and offer support if anyone needed it. We instructed students to record notes in their journals on any information that stood out to them. The museum is self-guided, so students could explore at his/her preferred pace. The beginning of the museum display shows maps detailing the populations of tribes prior to Westward Expansion, and then shows maps throughout the following years. It covers information on the many treaties presented to tribal members by the U.S. government, and then details the ways in which the treaties were broken. Students then begin reading about wars on the plains and the history of Wounded Knee. The Wounded Knee section shows photographs of the victims and quotes by people who survived. The final display shows the medals and accolades that the U.S. government soldiers received for their role in the massacre.

Students displayed a variety of responses to the information. My observational notes recorded that some students read each and every piece of information, while others only read certain sections. I also described three students who began crying quietly while reading the Wounded Knee stories. All students displayed signs of anger when reaching the display of government medals of honor. Some students began to write in their journals, while sitting on the floor in front of the display. One student turned to me and hugged me. After reading a few of the stories told by victims, two students, both male, stopped reading altogether and went and sat down to wait for the rest of us.

When analyzing the experience through student journals and interviews, I found that student responses showed feelings of anger, sadness, and "shutting down" at the time of the experience. The following responses were recorded during individual reflection time, prior to any group discussion.

Anger was evident in Beth's journal:

> It is disgusting that they have memorials for murderers. It makes me sick that they wouldn't even give the Indians they "captured" the chance to bury their dead.

Faith faces the information with a mixture of shock and anger:

> To me, what happened at Wounded Knee was a horribly ruthless display of human slaughter. I don't understand how our government could be so cold as to kill hundreds of innocent people and then congratulate the soldiers for "a well done job". It's sick and heartless! I would have never known about any of this, if not for this trip, and that upsets me.

Multicultural educators and social justice educators recognize that exposing all sides and views of an issue creates crisis (Kumashiro, 2004; Adams, Bell, and Griffin, 1997). For Faith, the crisis came in two forms—the truth that her own government allowed this to happen, and the distress that the topic isn't being taught in school. Faith was not the only student to respond in this way. As recorded in my journal, Mary came to me in the museum gift shop and said very quickly and with a harsh tone, "Why didn't I know about this before? This is a genocide that happened right here in the U.S.—everybody should know about this!"

I responded, "That's part of the problem, right? The text books and the way we are educated often show only part of the story."

"Yeah," she replied, "It's like you have to dig for the truth. What if some people don't want to do the digging? It's just wrong that schools wouldn't teach us this. All they talk about is how great America is."

This conversation demonstrated that students felt that there was something missing from their previous history courses. Prior to arriving at our alternative school, most of our students experienced history only through the textbook. Loewen (2010) writes that textbooks often focus on the progress of America and leave out anything that may be perceived in a negative way. Textbooks usually ignore the nadir of race relations, the period of time from 1890 to 1940 when things got progressively worse for Native Americans, African Americans, Chinese Americans, and Mexican Americans—the time period when the Wounded Knee massacre took place (Loewen, 2010, p. 189). Our students displayed feelings of distress over the fact that they never discussed anything about this in other classes. When they returned to school, students began reflecting on their class curriculum and speaking about what needs to change within them. As one history teacher in our building told me, "Kids from your trip question everything now. They are always looking for more to the story." As Valdez (2002) writes:

> In order for multicultural diversity (education) to be effective at the transformational level the teacher needs to have the courage to teach sensitive material and issues about oppression, discrimination, and racism as they really exist not only in society but also within the very institutions where they are taught. (Valdez, 2002, ¶ 4).

As high school educators, we recognize that Wounded Knee is just one of the many stories missing from history classes. We recognize that our educational institutions need to change. The fact that our students began recognizing this, speaking about it, and advocating for it upon their return to school is a significant example of transformational learning.

Another response to the Wounded Knee Museum was that some students partially "shut down." Two of the boys stopped reading and walked outside. One of them was agitated and asking for a cigarette. The other was joking and asking for lunch. But their agitation and walking away didn't mean that the moment was insignificant. Greg, one of the boys who stopped reading early, said in an interview when asked what events on the trip were significant:

The Wounded Knee Museum. I never really knew the truth about Wounded
Knee. That got me real depressed. It disgusted me that people could do that.
And I shouldn't have quit reading, but I did.

Greg's response supported Kumashiro's (2001) statement, "Learning
about oppression and unlearning what we had previously learned is
normal and normative can be upsetting" (pp. 8–9). In fact, some people object to teaching about human rights violations such as
Wounded Knee because they are too horrific or too controversial for
students. Other researchers question the motivation for teaching
about human rights violations, such as criticism of the Holocaust curriculum *Facing History and Ourselves* being marketed as psycho-social
development or character education (Maxwell, 2008). *Facing History
and Ourselves* states in their annual report:

> Facing History and Ourselves helps young people and adults make the con-
> nection between history and their own lives. We give educators professional
> development, support, and resources for teaching history and ethics.
> Through rigorous investigation of the events that led to the Holocaust, as
> well as other recent examples of hatred and violence, students in a Facing
> History class learn to combat prejudice with compassion, indifference with
> participation, and myth and misinformation with knowledge…Facing His-
> tory inspires students all over the globe to take responsibility for their
> world. (Facing History and Ourselves Annual Report-About Us)

According to the annual report, there was evidence of transformative
learning (Facing History and Ourselves). But Maxwell's (2008) work
raises a good question—does the marketing of a program influence
the transformative learning experienced by educators and students?
Does having a goal with a set outcome involving character education
create additional complexities within power structures within a classroom? Cranton's work on transformative learning (2006) addresses
power. She encourages educators to "unmask or question their understanding of power and examine their practice carefully for ways in
which power is hidden behind surface forms that appear to be free"
(p. 110). In our case, it is important to note that we built the Wounded
Knee experience into our curriculum, not as a point of character education, but as an element of multicultural education. Showing both

sides of this historical event through the power of the first-person ac-
counts by both government officials and Native American victims
was planned because of our belief in Banks's second dimension of
multicultural education—teaching students that our ideas and beliefs
about historical events are based upon cultural frames that shape in-
terpretations of history (Banks, 2004). We only became aware of the
transformational aspects of the Wounded Knee Museum experience
after our first visit. Cranton's (2006) conversations about power, and
Maxwell's (2008) questioning of program goals are important, as we
must continue to be honest about our motivations. Are we expecting
students to respond in a certain way through this experience? Now
that we know the power of the experience, are we "using" it to per-
petuate an ideal transformative experience? We will continue to ask
ourselves these important questions as we move forward.

Another example of transformative learning is that for some
White students the Wounded Knee Museum transformed their thinking about their White identity. Jackie wrote the following in her journal:

> Everything I've learned makes me think about whites in a whole new per-
> spective, like I've been given a whole new way to look at the world. I don't
> think this trip is all about Native Americans—it's about trying to find who
> you are and how you fit into your world, how you react when the elements
> are testing you, seeing how you react to the world around you.

Suzy said in an interview when asked about Wounded Knee:

> I actually felt ashamed of being White. I was very ashamed that even some-
> body could do that. And knowing that they, like me... I probably would
> have, if I was brought up during that time. I probably would have been a
> part of the group that was doing all of that just because of the color of my
> skin. I felt ashamed that people like me just did that.

Suzy may have been moving through one of the statuses of Helms's
White Racial Identity Development Model (Helms, 1984). According
to Helms, "racial identity" refers to a sense of group or collective
identity based on one's perception that he or she shares a common
racial heritage with a particular racial group (Helms and Carter, 1990,

p. 3). In the White Racial Identity model, Whites potentially develop five statuses (originally called stages). Helms and Carter (1990) went on to develop the White Identity Attitude Scale, a scale used to assess racial identity schemas. The schemas include the following for Whites:

- Contact, believing that they are "color blind" and are oblivious to racism and a denial of the meaning of race in one's life
- Disintegration, feeling conflicted over racial issues perceived as "moral dilemmas" and confused about the social rules of White socialization
- Reintegration—a belief in White superiority and the recognition of oneself belonging to the White group
- Psuedo-Independence-characterized by an intellectual awareness of white privileges
- Autonomy—defined as a nonracist identification of the White group

Helms (1990, 1997) proposed an additional schema called Immersion-Emersion. In this schema, Whites begin actively exploring what it means to be White. They search for examples of how they benefit from White privilege and reflect on their personal meaning of racism.

After Wounded Knee, Suzy seemed to move into the Psuedo-Independence stage. Helms wrote that a person is likely to enter this phase due to a painful or insightful encounter. For Suzy, experiencing the Wounded Knee museum, learning about the decimation of the bison and hearing the story of Crazy Horse's life and death were all described as knowledge that "hurt her heart." Helms also states that, in this schema, the person begins trying to understand racial differences and may reach out to people of color. Suzy showed evidence of this by asking students of color more questions and carrying on conversations with them about her feelings.

Suzy and Jackie also shared their feelings during Circle, enabling them to process even more. Transformational learning theorists, as well as multicultural educators, stress the important role that discourse plays in transforming ideas and beliefs. Mezirow (2000) describes discourse in the context of Transformation Theory in the following way:

> That specialized use of dialogue devoted to searching for a common understanding and assessment of the justification of an interpretation or belief...Reflective discourse involves a critical assessment of assumptions. It leads toward a clearer understanding by tapping collective experience to arrive at a tentative best judgment (pp. 10–11).

For Suzy and Jackie, time spent in Circle enabled them to learn that other White students were experiencing similar responses to the museum. In addition, Suzy and Jackie reached out to us as teachers, and we were able to share experiences that shifted our beliefs about our own Whiteness, such as the first times we became aware of our privileges and the first times that we experienced painful associations with our Whiteness. The transformations in both young women seemed to have a lasting effect. After the trip, Suzy participated in clubs, such as the Multicultural Club, and continued to explore her feelings about being White. She volunteered and attended fundraisers such as walks to benefit others. Jackie says that she "spoke out more" after the trip regarding issues of race.

It was not just White students undergoing changes in their belief systems. As a whole, the trip also caused transformations in students of color regarding their ethnic identity. According to Yinger (1976), ethnic identity is viewed as an individual's identification with a "segment of a larger society whose members are thought, by themselves or others, to have a common origin and share segments of a common culture" (p. 200). Phinney (1990) writes that there are four significant components of ethnic identity for education:

1. Self-identification—how one sees oneself.
2. Positive and negative attitudes towards one's group leading to pride and pleasure, or denial of ethnic identity and feelings of inferiority.
3. Sense of belonging—related to the experience of exclusion or detachment from one's own or dominant group.

4. Sensitivity to specific cultural practice—educators may need to
   have a knowledge of history and culture in order to understand
   individual groups and their experiences. (pp. 9–13)

The connections that people make regarding their ethnicity are also
very important. Chavez and Guido-DiBrito (1999) state:

> These points of connection allow individuals to make sense of the world
> around them and to find pride in who they are. If, however, positive ethnic
> group messages and support are not apparent to counter-act negative public
> messages, a particular individual is likely to feel shame or disconnection
> toward their own ethnic identity. (p. 41)

Margaret, an Ojibwe student, experienced these points of connection. Throughout the trip, we saw Margaret begin to actively engage
in stories of Native American people. She became a voracious reader
and was often reading Native American poetry or writings in the van
during the drive. Responding passionately to the stories of Sitting
Bull and Crazy Horse, she wrote journals detailing her feelings of
pride regarding the courage of Native people. Her responses supported the studies that found that multicultural materials have a positive influence on Native American students, as well as English
Language Learners (Villegas and Lucas, 2007). Gay (2000) writes that
teachers must engage in *culturally responsive* teaching. Culturally responsive teachers work to incorporate practices that affirm their students' identities and teach to the diversity of learning styles present in
their classrooms. Culturally responsive teachers also believe that a
child's culture shapes who they are and that culture merits space
within the curriculum. We considered all of this when preparing the
curriculum for our students such as Margaret. Garrett and Garrett
(1994) describe the significance of humor, family and elders in their
overview of Native American cultural values. By incorporating aspects of Margaret's culture, such as storytelling, using humor, preparing sage offerings, using fire to create a space for conversation, and
the readings of Native American people, she felt safe to learn. In addition, in an interview she speaks of a transformation that she went
through regarding her racial identity:

I knew a little bit about my culture, but not a whole lot. The curriculum shaped me. To an extent it made me realize how far we've come since then and what we had to do to survive. I liked to hear the stories and talk to the Native American artists at the Crazy Horse monument. I related to the story of Crazy Horse, how he wasn't always a warrior and was once shy. I remember Crazy Horse, and all the things he did, how he got his name, and everything about him. I wanted to learn everything I could.

Margaret also responded to the injustices that she learned about and her awareness that they still exist:

Native people got treated so bad. We were always misjudged. We still are. Especially on reservations and cities around them. The stereotypes…in some ways, not much has changed. It's sad but they weren't treated very well. [pause] But people like me can break the stereotypes down.

Margaret spoke of her experience visiting the Bighorn Medicine Wheel. The 700-year-old Medicine Wheel, located high up in the Bighorn Mountains, was a visit that we made each year. The large wheel is made of gathered rocks, and twenty-eight spokes radiate out to a rim of about eighty feet (Brockman, 1998). Students hiked among clouds and mountains to the sacred site. There, students such as Margaret participated in sage offerings. She describes the experience:

There aren't many words to describe how it felt. Amazing, but that still doesn't put it into words, how it felt. It was just a totally different experience to be there and feel it. Because it's like *my people*. It was just amazing. I felt connected. I was definitely emotional. Even though my grandma had never been there, I just felt like she was there with me.

This connection to her family roots was something that Margaret still speaks of six years after she first visited the Medicine Wheel. "It stays with me, you know," she said in a recent interview. "I can't wait to show my daughter the same things."

And she did. She and her husband took their daughter on a trip that mirrored ours this last summer. "It was amazing to be back there, showing all of the things to my family. There were so many memories from the trip. I still felt connected to you guys."

Interestingly, in the midst of learning about topics like Wounded Knee, Margaret was transformed through what she calls "forgiveness":

> I remember opening up a lot to everyone and being on a new level with everyone. What I remember most on the first trip was that we were learning how to forgive people. Because who would have thought that you'd learn about forgiving, on a camping trip? But you did, you know.

When asked for more details, she said:

> I learned to forgive people who hurt me in the past, our history...I don't know, just everything.

Without the trusting relationships that developed as a result of Circle, Suzy and Jackie may not have openly discussed their feelings of guilt and shame. Margaret may not have gotten to share her feelings of pride or forgiveness. Transformational learning theorists, multicultural education theorists, social justice educators, human rights educators, and restorative justice practitioners all stress that feelings of trust and security are essential elements for encouraging free full participation in discourse (Mezirow, 2009; Taylor, 2009; Tibbitts, 2005; Adams, Bell, and Griffin, 1997, p. 49; and Boyes-Watson, 2008.). Cranton writes in *Understanding and Promoting Transformative Learning*: "Equal participation and freedom from coercion are central to discourse serving as a vehicle for empowerment" (p. 124). Circle allows students to have access to equal participation and the freedom to "pass" if they weren't moved to speak. In addition, researchers in these areas also stress the importance of relationships in the process (Nieto, 1992, p. 48; Taylor, 2000, p. 307; and Ukpokodu, 2009). Because we focused on content integration when we developed the curriculum, and because we used Circle to foster feelings of safety, students were able to not only explore their feelings about the "retelling of history," they were also able to experience transformations regarding their racial and ethnic identities. But what happens if trust and security are not present in the classroom when difficult topics are presented?

The responses of Jackie and Suzy raise important questions regarding the teaching of difficult topics. First, what if a teacher was teaching this information in an oppressive environment? Bell and Griffin (1997) write:

> The way students experience the environment of the classroom has a powerful effect on whether or not they are willing to entertain conflicting information and internal disequilibrium. If the environment is perceived as threatening, a person's defenses may be fairly rigid. They will tend to ignore challenges to their worldview and any conflicting information will be rationalized to fit the present belief system. If the environment is perceived as supportive, a person's defenses may be more permeable...We want to construct an environment that is supportive and trustworthy, one in which uncomfortable and challenging issues may be raised and explored, where students can express discomfort, confusion, anger, and fear and know they will be treated with dignity and respect. (p. 49)

Angel reflects on what we did as educators to promote trust and respect:

> I feel as though we gave our students a platform to use their voice, be their true selves, and allowed them to be an equal within our group. Creating an environment that did not tolerate foul language or disrespect gave students room to be themselves and to feel respected. We tried to offer students an opportunity like they had never had before and model for them what respect looked like. I feel as though the students respected us, as staff, because we held everyone accountable, including ourselves, without doing it in a disrespectful or punitive way. By having clear expectations and appropriate boundaries it fostered a learning environment where respect became second nature. From there, exploration and fun occurred because we didn't have to focus on things like safety issues or disrespect.

Angel's statement that we, as educators, held ourselves accountable for promoting a respectful environment is significant. We modeled these norms with each other as well. In my experience, educators often don't display supportive and respectful behavior towards each other, which trickles down and impacts students. We made sure that everything we did to ensure that students felt safe and respected, we did with each other as well.

As noted in Chapter Three, many of our students did not feel comfortable in their traditional classrooms. They distrusted adults in their schools and felt like outsiders. One of our students of color said: "I felt uncomfortable a lot in my classes and would just walk out. Especially when we were reading about slavery. Then I'd get in trouble for it." It is probable that many other students feel those same feelings. So what happens to those students when difficult subjects are presented? Does the experience just lead to further disengagement with school? And what if teachers aren't aware that students may be feeling guilt or shame as a result of a classroom experience? What if teachers don't stop to acknowledge any of their students' emotional responses to subject matter? What if teachers don't feel prepared or comfortable handling the topics? Indeed, researchers note that, "Emotions are an integral part of how teachers view their roles, yet when it comes to the preparation and development of pre-service and in-service teachers, the function of emotions in the classroom tends to be either ignored or relegated to a minor status" (Williams et al., 2008). Teachers in all subject matters need to be aware of the wide array of emotional responses and need to be prepared to support their students throughout the process. If not, opportunities for transformational learning decrease. More research needs to be conducted on the effects of the teaching of difficult topics in unsupportive classrooms, especially in secondary school.

Another important question is how do teachers continue to support their students after they have completed their classes? As a SEED student, I personally felt isolation after my classes ended. I felt the sting of loneliness in the work and felt that others, even my own family, just couldn't understand the transformation that I had undergone. I had to work hard to contact people from my group and visit with them so that I felt connected to a social justice community. Manglitz, Johnson-Bailey, and Cervero (2005), when interviewing White adult educators who challenge racism, found that the educators often felt alienation and had to find a community of support. If we feel this way as adults, imagine what young people feel like after going through transformational learning regarding race, class, and gender issues.

Randy, Angel, and I recognized that students continued to grapple with questions raised by experiences like Wounded Knee long after the trip ended. As teachers, we continued to support students in their discoveries once they returned to school the following year. For example, I hosted a multicultural/human rights club in which we worked through complex issues using excerpts from Cushner's workbook, *Human Diversity in Action* (2003). Students kept journals of their own intercultural experiences, participated in field trips where they interviewed people from different cultures (p. 151), learned terms such as *ethnocentrism, objective culture*, and *subjective culture*. They also wrote a list of twenty "I am _____" statements through Cushner's (2003) *Who Am I* activity (p. 55) and completed the Examining Stereotypes activity (p. 157). Students from the trip were club leaders who led discussions during meetings. They showed leadership in numerous ways, such as recruiting others, questioning stereotypes, and openly talking about how their ideas about race and culture were transformed during the Westward Bound course.

Randy, Angel, and I were also advisors to some of our students, so we saw them daily in an Advisory course. We recognized the limitations of our program, however. In many instances, Randy, Angel, and I said, "We've got to get them back together again." A few students graduated after the trip or weren't in our courses, and regrettably, we weren't able to offer daily support as they continued moving forward in the development of their multicultural identities. We did conduct a reunion Circle for our third-year students, which was a huge success. One goal moving forward is to provide further courses for veterans of our program and invitations to Circle so that students can continue to feel our support as they move on in their adult lives.

Prejudice Reduction—Racism and Circle

Banks's next dimension is prejudice reduction. Banks describes prejudice reduction as the extent to which teachers and administrators actively work to reduce prejudice and stereotyping. In addition to the curriculum previously mentioned, we used our time in Circle to openly discuss prejudice and stereotyping. We defined stereotyping and then asked, "What types of stereotypes were present in the newspaper articles written during this time?" and "What types of stereotypes are present in our media today?" We also spoke openly about labels and the negative effects that they can have on communities. Our students had personal experience in being labeled and stereotyped because of their clothing, intelligence, class rank, race, religion, and socio-economic backgrounds. Ghosh and Abdi (2004) write that youth who do not share the same characteristics as the powerful are "different" and this difference may serve as the basis for discrimination. They argue:

> It is important that teachers, along with the students, examine new ways to understand how power works in constructing race, class, and gender, and how power differentials are maintained through racism, sexism, and classism…Even if they want to, educators in today's pluralistic societies cannot escape from their responsibility to discuss racism, sexism, stereotypes, prejudice, and discrimination, all of which play an important role in constructing the we-and-they relations. (p. 80)

Our Circles provided a safe place for students and staff to talk about the pain that they felt when they were labeled or discriminated against and to examine the ways that power relationships impacted our lives. Thus, when we began speaking of stereotypes within the history that we were presenting, students were able to feel empathy for the groups that we studied. They were also developing questions such as, "What can I do about racism and classism?" and "What's my responsibility in all of this?"

Reducing prejudice does not come easily nor is it without conflict. During our 2006 trip, a significant conflict arose between an African American student and White students regarding the use of racial slurs. We had been driving for about two hours and had just stopped the van at an art museum. One of the girls, an African American, got out of the van and looked upset. I had been driving in the other van, so Angel and I approached her to ask her what was going on. She stated that some students were telling jokes during the drive and were using racial slurs. The joking students were in the back seat of the van, so Randy didn't hear what had been said. After talking with our student for a few minutes, I asked her if she felt comfortable gathering together in Circle to talk through the event. She agreed and we held a Circle. During Circle, each individual shared his/her role in the incident, was asked what he/she thought about using racial slurs, and was asked to share their feelings about it. Randy and I were participants in the Circle and shared our thoughts and feelings as well.

I was able to separately interview two of the students five months after the event. I begin with the victim's reflection about that Circle and will honor her words and will include the complete text of this phase in the interview:

> Student: Like we were in the van and I think it was (lists students) and I was sitting there and I remember two people started telling jokes about black people and stuff. And someone else joined in. And they were saying, "There's a difference in being a nigger and a *nigger*." And like it just made me feel uncomfortable. You know, I'm thinking, "I'm forced to be in this space with these people and can't get away from it." At that moment I was thinking, "I'm done. I don't want to be around these people. Send me to the other van." Umm. Like we resolved it. It was a good situation. I kind of felt like they didn't understand why it upset me, but they had stopped doing it and I settled for that. We're here for ten days and I can't be mad the whole time.

> Amy: Do you feel that justice was restored?

> Student: Umm. Kind of, because then they could understand, or I could at least tell them, how it made me feel. I don't really know how they took it personally. The only way I think it would have truly made things better is if they felt why I was upset and that they understood it instead of, "Oh, I understand and don't want to get in trouble."

> Amy: Do you think that when some of them chose to speak openly about their role in the joking, did that validate anything?

> Student: Yeah. A little bit. It wasn't just like I'm a whiny little baby and just shut up. For them to admit that they were wrong kind of made me feel better because at least they know that it was their fault somehow.

> Amy: Is there anything that the teachers did that was helpful or harmful in that situation?

Student: I don't think anything was harmful. Something was done about it right away. Because the way that I felt, I was just gonna ignore it, and I probably would have blown up on someone eventually. I think that was probably the best solution, looking back on it. Having this instant action and you guys just snapped into it having that "No way, not on my trip!" kind of thing [smiles].

Amy: Do you think Circle could ever restore justice in terms of racism?

Student: Umm. I don't think so. I just think it's something that's so institutionalized and it's something that's passed on from so many years. I don't think there's one thing that can make it stop or make it better. I just remember after the Circle I just wanted to go in and look at the cool stuff in the museum.

This conversation raises questions about the use of Circle in conflict-resolution situations, especially those involving issues of race, class, and gender. Though the student felt that no harm was done, and was able to enjoy the museum afterwards, she clearly recognized the limitations of Circle restoring justice in terms of institutional racism.

The perpetrator speaks of the Circle as being highly significant and transformational for her. Without prompting, she brought up this Circle when asked if there was a Circle that stood out for her:

And I remember one, when we were riding in the van and a couple of students, I was involved with it, were talking about racist jokes. And to us, we thought it was just funny and we didn't really think anything of it. And we were going to a museum, I forgot what it was called, and we had to sit around. And our group, those in our van, had to sit around in Circle while the others went in the museum, and we had to talk about how racism is bad and even if it was jokes, it does hurt people. And I guess I really never looked at it in a way to where, you know, I could hurt someone's feelings, even if it was jokes, cuz you know there's white jokes out there, and all different kinds of things. But, the way that you said how you had many experiences with kids and everything, it just made me look at it in a different perspective. And it really changed my point, and even to this day I don't really say racist jokes anymore. I won't. Cuz I do actually think about that Circle a lot. That was really actually one of the most powerful Circles that I guess that I've ever had. Or interventions, really [smiles].

Amy: When you say intervention, how was that Circle experience different than if somebody would have just...[Amy pauses]

Student: Came at me in a different way? [smiles] Well, actually I mean we got in trouble for it, but it seemed more like you could understand where we were coming from, but you also made us look at it in a different person's point of view. And, how to explain it...it didn't make me not want to say it in front of you, and just go and say it behind your back. You really made us think about it, to where you wouldn't want us to just say it period. To where it's really not good to say racist jokes, even if you mean it in a funny way, it can still hurt people's feelings. It can still hit someone in a certain spot and they won't show it, but you really hurt them in a certain way. And it just, I don't know, it's hard to explain how it was different, but it just really hit me, that Circle I guess.

Amy: How were you feeling at the start of the Circle and then throughout to the end?

Student: In the beginning, I felt really embarrassed: I felt like, "Oh, she caught me." And I didn't really mean to hurt anyone's feelings and that I didn't want to get in trouble. I thought I was going to get in huge trouble by the teachers and maybe get sent home or something. I felt really super embarrassed and I didn't want to really say anything. And then I noticed how... everyone just wasn't saying anything, and I was looking around and I knew I had started the jokes, so I came out and said, "You know it was me that said something." At the end, I felt more comfortable. I felt better about myself that I actually came out and said something. I actually felt really good and that I actually understood things, I guess. Cuz at the beginning, I was just really embarrassed. And at the end, I felt a lot more comfortable.

What is significant about the student's reflection is that she mainly discussed how my participation in Circle impacted her, not the other students' sharing (including the victim). In that Circle, Randy and I both voiced our personal feelings about racial slurs and racial jokes, and shared the hurt that the words made us feel. But the second student never mentioned learning from the first student's pain. In this case, the White student learned from the White teacher, not from the African American student who was victimized. This also may offer insight into relationships of power and limitations of Circle. Though Randy and I sat in Circle equal to the students, and shared our past personal stories regarding racial slurs rather than lecturing about that specific incident, did our students view us as the authority figures? Even though Chapter Three showed evidence of students rethinking their ideas of us as people, not just teachers, this instance clearly demonstrates that the student may have been listening to teachers more than the other students. Thus, does the use of conflict-resolution Circles only enhance the power structure of teacher as authority? Was the Circle just another documentation on White privilege and oppression? Though the African American student chose to participate and said that the Circle helped her in some way, could the Circle have had the same impact without requiring the African American student to share her pain? Notice that the African American student also used the words "settled for it" when describing the result. What additional hurts were still buried?

Much more research in the area of restorative justice Circles and racism and prejudice needs to be pursued. Though I responded immediately to the incident as a teacher and tied that incident to educational discussions on other racial slurs used today and in 1890, I still felt the self-doubt that I hadn't done enough. Many White educators feel these struggles and self-doubts, but those who continue to directly "call people to task" and hold others accountable challenge racism (Manglitz, Johnson-Bailey, and Cervero, 2005, p. 1265). From this experience I learned that prejudice reduction through both curriculum and discourse methods, such as Talking Circles, needs to be carried out carefully so that it is not always the student of color responding to the prejudice. (When the Circle has limited students of color, care must be taken so that the students of color aren't viewed as a spokesperson for their race.) Circle should also not be used solely to "educate the oppressors," as it may end up not helping the people of color. Also, the teacher must be aware of his/her role in the Circle and that students may still view him/her as the authority on the subject. Perhaps this was a Circle in which Randy and I should have been more passive participants. This type of reflection is necessary on the part of Circle facilitators so that they recognize the strengths and limitations of the process.

Equity Pedagogy

The fourth dimension is equity pedagogy—pedagogies designed specifically to increase the academic achievement of lower-performing students and to create greater equity among students (Banks and Banks, 1995). The alternative school and the programs within it were focused on increasing academic achievements of lower performing students. Indeed, some evidence shows that alternative schools can help keep students in school (Dynarski and Wood, 1997; Franklin et al., 2007; Washington State Institute, 2009). As instructors we also focused on providing experiences that all students could participate in. We did so by fundraising to make all opportunities free of fees for students. Also, we actively sought ways to enable students with medical conditions, such as diabetes and pregnancy, to safely attend our trips. In addition, we focused on engaging students with disabilities. We also valued students who spoke English as a second language by inviting students to share aspects of their culture, speak their first language, and teach other students about their language. Soon Hmong students were teaching us greetings, phrases, and pieces of their culture. On their own, they also cooked a Hmong meal over the campfire for all of us the final night and taught our group that in Hmong culture, cooking and eating together is a way to give thanks. All of these steps helped to create equity among students.

The last dimension, empowering school culture by altering school structures and processes and focusing on eliminating institutionalized racism, is still a work in progress. We did focus on empowering school culture by inviting students who participated in our program to become leaders in our building upon their return to school. In many cases, students became involved in student council, a leadership class, or a human rights club. On an individual level, the trip itself empowered students to vocalize their concerns regarding racism. As far as altering school structures, our program was one example of that. We advocated for a summer enrichment program, because we were unable to conduct the program during the school year. I began researching because I wanted clear data to present to other school programs, showing that time should be created during the school year for programs like these. This work continues. It is often difficult for districts to incorporate programs like ours because of the inflexibility of scheduling, school structures, and the fears associated with taking students labeled "at-risk" out of their school buildings. We continue to work on raising awareness about this issue and continue to advocate for change within educational institutions.

Culturally Relevant Practices

In addition to the work of Banks, our multicultural foundation was supported by Ladson-Billings's (1994) concept of culturally relevant practices. Ladson-Billings writes that culturally relevant teachers have high self-esteem and a high regard for others, see teaching as an art, and see teaching as giving back to communities. Randy, Angel, and I all shared these philosophies. In addition, we believed that all of our students could succeed. We displayed that belief in our practice—our belief that all of our students could succeed, our care for each as an individual, and our use of evening Talking Circles allowed students to feel validated. In an interview, Suzy said, "Because you guys—Bauer, Salathe and you—believed in me, I started to believe in me too."

Ladson-Billings (1994) also writes that culturally relevant practices include helping students make connections with their community, national, and global identities. We believe strongly in this practice and used Human Rights Education as a foundation for building these connections.

Human Rights Education

In addition to multicultural education, Human Rights Education had a great impact on our students. Human Rights Education is defined as all learning that develops the knowledge, skills, and values of human rights (Flowers, 1997). HRE includes teaching *about* human rights such as providing the history of the rights and information about human rights violations, as well as teaching *for* human rights, which encourages a responsibility for protecting and defending human rights (Flowers, 1997). Human Rights Education (HRE) serves multiple purposes. One purpose of HRE is to promote and advocate for the universal right of access to education, the right to quality education, and the right to respect within the learning community (UNICEF, 2007). A UNICEF report states that, "A comprehensive rights-based approach must be dynamic, accounting for different learning environments and different learners" (UNICEF, 2007). Our Westward Bound program was one way that we could provide quality education for learners who learned differently than the lecture methods used in traditional classrooms.

Reardon (1995/1997) writes that a second principle of HRE is focused on human dignity—its recognition, fulfillment, and universalization. In addition, HRE is a vehicle for studying positive peace and nonviolent conflict resolution (Reardon, 1995/1997). Though HRE is a relatively new field in education, educators are choosing to incorporate it because it promotes democratic principles, helps to develop communications skills and critical thinking, engages the heart and mind, and affirms the interdependence of the human community (Flowers, 1997).

Additional principles of HRE, as written in *Human Rights Here and Now* (1998), a collection of writings published by the Human Rights Educators' Network, shaped our program:

1. Open-mindedness: We modeled this and expected our students to display open-mindedness with each other, the curriculum, and the experiences of the trip.
2. International and Global Focus: Though the curriculum focused on Westward Expansion, we also guided discussions on forced relocations currently happening in places such as Darfur.
3. Positive Value Systems: Though much of our curriculum brought human rights abuses towards indigenous people directly in front of our students, we also emphasized human rights in a positive way, such as spending a day in service at *Meeting the Need*, a camp in the Black Hills that provides opportunities for people with disabilities to enjoy an outdoor Black Hills experience.
4. Providing evidence that individuals can make a difference: We did this by introducing students to individuals who are making a difference in their communities. Students listened as Dallas Dietrich, the founder of *Meeting the Need*, shared the story of an auto accident that disabled him. They listened with great attention

as he explained why he began advocating for outdoor experiences for people with disabilities rather than just "giving up on life." Students also viewed the film of sculptor Korczak Ziolkowski and Chief Henry Standing Bear, the men who started the Crazy Horse Memorial in June of 1948. Students were moved by the resilience of Ziolkowski's family and their commitment to continue work on the monument year after year. These stories of advocacy, determination, and care for others provided evidence that an individual can make a huge difference in the world.

5. Making connections to the Universal Declaration of Human Rights: We took care to point out connections with our experiences and curriculum to the UDHR. We asked questions such as, "What human rights have been violated?" or "What needed to change to protect the human rights of those involved?"

6. Cultural diversity: As previously described, we ensured that diversity was present in activities and curriculum.

7. Participatory Methods: We provided a large variety of engaging strategies and experiences, such as hands-on learning, Circle, and experiences with nature and animals.

8. Making connections: We constantly made connections between our experiences, the UDHR, current events, literature, history, and environmental advocacy. (Flowers, 1997)

The Advocates for Human Rights, a nonprofit organization based in Minneapolis, Minnesota, trained Randy, Angel, and me on ways to incorporate HRE into our teaching. In an interview with the program's Education Program Associate, Kathy Seipp, I asked Ms. Seipp why HRE is important. She stated:

I feel that HRE is important in many ways and on multiple levels, both from the global to the local and the intrinsic to the extrinsic. Children naturally like to learn about people and places other than what they are familiar with and HRE can broaden their world. HRE also directly links to the lives of your students and by making this connection for them we are helping them reframe their paradigm. For example, instead of the routine language and consequences for punishing a student who is teasing another student in class, you could say something to the effect of by continually bothering

Johnny, not only are you hurting his feelings but you are infringing on his right to education, as stated article #26 of the UDHR. We all have an equal right to an education. While you are in this classroom the rights of all students must be protected and we each have a role to play and our responsible for our own actions.

"Reframing their paradigm" is a phrase that resonates with me. In the case of the racist jokes, one of the discussion points that I was able to make was: "Listening to racial slurs violates a person's right to security. How does racist language infringe on a person's security? Or how might it impact students' right to education?" Students were then able to discuss their ideas. Being able to use the language of the UDHR shifts student awareness—it moves an issue from being a subjective "morality issue" of right or wrong, into an issue of international rights. It moves students beyond the idea that a teacher is just telling them something that he or she believes, into a realm of understanding that these articles were ratified and that the wording of the document was voted on over 1400 times! It allows students to move beyond their own experiences and begin to reflect on the experiences of others. For example Adrienne said in an interview: "Human rights is about so much more than you or me. It's about doing what is right for everybody."

Students had a variety of positive responses when asked about Human Rights Education in a post-program interview. When asked why Human Rights Education is important, Greg said: "I think it is important because it makes you look at different cultures and their habits more. Violating the rights of people is wrong—everybody deserves to do what they want as long as they don't harm others."

Margaret had this to say about Human Rights Education:

I think that it's very important for others to learn about human rights violations, especially school aged kids. I feel like it just gets kinda passed by by some teachers so people don't really get to see the perspective of the innocent victims who had to go through the struggles they had to go though. I think when you learn about it you kind of have more of an open mind about others and their feelings, as well as the things they go through. So I guess it makes you more sensitive to others' needs and wants.

Adrienne said:

> Human Rights Education is so important. There's so much hurt going on in
> the world right now. It opened my eyes to things that I just didn't know
> about. Now I look for those things. And I read about them. I also feel like
> fighting back. It takes some of my angsty-energy and puts it to good use.

Adrienne's response echoed Ms. Seipp's:

> When children of any age realize the impact of their own actions on others
> both at home and afar, we have done our job as human rights educators by
> lighting that spark to initiate a desire to continue to learn about ourselves
> and find our place in the world. It is the role of a human rights educator to
> not only to facilitate the discovery of the rights we have as human beings
> but also to realize the responsibility that comes with it. Students like to par-
> ticipate in HRE because it's real. So much of school life as told to students is
> to prepare them for the *real world* in the future and HRE allows them to be a
> part of something that is real in their lives *now*. They might participate in a
> food drive, visit and work at a shelter, raise money for a cause of their
> choice ...by taking part in activities that are real heightens the level of stu-
> dent engagement and gives it meaning.

Researchers agree with Ms. Seipp. According to Tibbits (2005),
"Human rights education is not merely about valuing and respecting
human rights, but about fostering personal action in order to guaran-
tee these conditions" (p. 107). The idea that action can be taken now,
and that we all have a responsibility for promoting Human Rights, is
something that we stressed with our students through service projects. In addition to just learning about Human Rights, students were
shown examples of how individuals can help promote rights. During
the 2006 trip, students worked on fire prevention at *Meeting the Need*,
the Black Hills camp being built for people with disabilities. We discussed that all people have the right to rest and leisure and the right
to enjoy natural settings. In both cases, students reflected positively
about their experiences. Faith said:

> Today was lots of fun. I thought it was really cool when we did the commu-
> nity service project. I didn't realize how strong everyone was and it really
> surprised me. It's amazing how everyone worked together so well. When
> Dallas told us his story, I felt like crying because nobody should have to go

through that. I think it's really cool how Dallas made a place where handi-
capped people can stay and admire the beautiful wilderness. That's very
nice. And it shows how you have to work hard to help others.

Jackie had similar things to say about the experience:

> Today we started out with doing a community service project. In the begin-
> ning, I didn't want to do anything when I found out we were going to bring
> logs and dead trees down a big steep hill. But as I started to work, for some
> reason I wanted to give it my all. I have cuts and bruises all over, but when
> Dallas stopped to talk to us and told his story, I felt an amazing sense of
> pride. And it felt so good, because we take advantage of so many little
> things that we can do, and it was a feeling I can't explain.

During two trips, students spent a day rebuilding campsites in
Wyoming while learning about environmental justice. Students were
disgusted by the amount of trash left near and within these campgrounds. Greg said, "I can't believe the trash people can just leave out
here. How do they expect the next person to come and enjoy themselves?" The Wyoming Forest Service staff told our students: "We
don't get much help out here. If you folks weren't able to do this,
things would just get left the way they are."

Hannah reflected on her community service experiences in her interview:

> It just makes me feel better to know that I can go back there almost at any
> time that I want to and say, "See that right there. I did that." It's not only
> about me, it's about other people too. Like when the park ranger said that
> the parks that you did last year, there's more people there. If it's better look-
> ing, then more people will want to be there. Nobody wants to live in a land-
> fill. When we pulled in there, I was thinking, "We're going to be working on
> THIS??? This is worth working on?" It was a hole! It was bad. But when
> we were done, it was pretty good. They could now take their horses out
> there and they wouldn't have their horses stepping in holes. And doing new
> fire rings—not having them is how forest fires start.

Hannah felt a sense of pride in the work that she did. In addition, she
pulled in her understanding of responsibility—she had helped prevent animal injuries and forest fires.

Mark reflected on his service project when asked what aspects of the trip that he would always remember. He said:

> Then the last thing has got to be community service. That was kind of hard. We had to move gravel and all that. We had to put a lot of back work into it, my back hurts! But after all that, you get to see what you've done, you get the satisfaction of seeing what you've done. You made an impact on the surroundings right there.

The connection between Human Rights Education, service-learning, and transformational learning is being researched today. Claus and Ogden (2004) state:

> Service learning is not simply a pedagogical innovation rooted in the principles of experiential education and an interest in helping people and organizations in need. It also has the potential to become a transformative social movement, but this will only be realized if we view it as such...at its best, service learning can create circumstances in which young people develop a deeper understanding of their world and themselves and an improved sense of purpose, justice, agency, and optimism. (pp. 69–70)

The positive aspects of service learning in our program were that students worked together and built relationships during the process. Clyde said: "I got to know about the strengths and weaknesses of our team. It felt good to help each other when a fallen tree was too big to carry by ourselves."

Margaret also spoke of helping one another:

> I was really excited and looking forward to doing them actually. It felt really good to do something. Even though it was part of the trip and we kind of had to do it, I never felt like we HAD to. No one was upset about having to do it. We rebuilt fire rings the first year and then rebuilt a horse camp the other. It didn't feel like we had to do it, it just felt like part of our learning experience. It was cool because we got to work together in teams, so we got to help each other out and see how the other person works under pressure. I think that our work was appreciated a lot.

Another positive aspect of our service projects is that they promoted the development of positive relationships with additional adults. For example, students worked side by side with two park rangers and four adult volunteers when rebuilding campgrounds. The adults took the time to engage with our students and told stories of their lives in Wyoming and the joys of working in nature. They shared a wonderful meal with our students as a "thank you." Students who generally wouldn't have trusted outside adults back at school openly shared information with our adult volunteers. Video footage of the day showed our students engaged in animated conversation, listening, and learning from these new elders. At our campfire Circle that night, students used words such as "awesome" and "wise" to describe the adults who helped them. In a post-trip interview, Greg said: "It was good to see other adults spending a day off working to help a beautiful place like that. They set a good example for me."

Other positive results included visible feelings of pride. These feelings were evident during our evening Circle. Students used storytelling to convey their experiences that day, what they learned about themselves, and how the day impacted them. Researchers stress the importance of reflection in service-learning opportunities (Hamilton and Fenzel, 1988; Rutter and Newmann, 1989; Yates and Youniss, 2004). Our students reflected positively in Circle and through journal entries.

Despite these positive results, there were clear limits to the power of service-learning within our program, in part due to travel and time constraints. Service-learning at its best is service that happens in the communities where students directly live and within programs where students are involved in selecting causes that they feel passionately about (Claus and Ogden, 2004). Due to the structure of our summer program, those elements did not take place. However, we are learning and adjusting as we build the program; and one key element that we would like to add is a service-learning class or club where our students serve as mentors to new students while they continue developing their own commitment to service.

Social Justice in Education

A final aspect of our program is that we teach using a social justice framework. Defining this becomes complex, as educational scholars disagree about the attributes and origins of social justice education, and often use additional terms to describe their work, such as multicultural education, postmodernism, antiracist education, and many more (North, 2008). Others argue that multicultural education and antiracist pedagogy differ greatly. Some researchers argue that multicultural education has become a slogan or catchphrase in schools that tends to tokenize the racially and economically oppressed and that too many hands have worked to make the curriculum "safe" for teachers, thus taking away some of the transformative power of the initial work (Giroux, 1994; Kailin, 2002). According to Kailin (2002), central elements of antiracist pedagogy are empowerment, a focus on the "relations of domination rather than on difference alone," and a focus on critically analyzing existing power relations and knowledge paradigms (pp. 54–55). Though much of our curriculum design fell under multicultural education, our discussions with students revolved around questions that fell under the umbrella of antiracist pedagogy and anti-oppressive pedagogy. For example, we held discussions about stereotypes. We asked students to discuss changes that they would make in schools to decrease suffering when students are labeled as "different." We also discussed oppression and each student identified oppression in history and in his or her lives today.

Kumashiro (2004) describes four overlapping approaches to anti-oppressive forms of education:

1. Improving the experiences of students who have traditionally been treated in harmful ways and not helpful ways.
2. Changing the knowledge that all students have about people in this world who have traditionally been labeled "different."
3. Challenging the broader and often invisible dynamics in society that privilege or favor certain groups and identities and marginalize or disadvantage others.
4. Recognizing that we (both as teachers and learners) often find comfort in the repetition of what is considered common sense. Educators need to invite students to address their own subconscious desires for learning only certain things and resistances to learning new things (p. xxxvii).

When speaking of social studies curriculum, for example, Kumashiro writes: "The task for teachers is not merely to add to the curriculum more information about different groups in society. The task is to ask questions about the political implications of the underlying story being told by whatever is included" (p. 62). Others note that social studies for social justice is about actively seeking the complexities associated with oppression and inequality and recognizing, as in the case of globalization, that the world is a "web of relationships" (Bigelow, 1990; and Bigelow and Peterson, 2002). Au (2009) writes that social studies for social justice centers around challenging the "hegemonic, status quo norms of historical knowledge" (¶ 4).

But what does all of that mean to a group of 16–19 year olds? We believe that evidence for their understanding of this was found most often in their journals or during their reflections in Circle. As previously stated, our students began asking questions about the missing stories and the connections between different stories. They also spoke about the dominant voices in the history of the West. One student wrote:

> I noticed that most of the news stories and blurbs in the museum were written by men with a big vocabulary. I imagine that they are wealthy and educated. So what was actually going on with the soldiers on the ground, or the dudes panning for gold?

Adams, Bell and Griffin (1997) write that, "Our goal in social justice education is to enable students to become conscious of their operating world view and to be able to examine critically alternative ways of understanding the world and social relations" (p. xvii). I believe that our students began this process on our trip. They may not have recognized why we asked the questions that we did, or understood those academic definitions of social justice education, but they did have thoughts and opinions about how the trip impacted their feelings about justice.

Promoting Justice for Students

In order to explore this topic, it was first important to try to determine what students' thoughts were about justice. When asked to define justice, students had a variety of responses. One student said, "My definition of justice is doing the right thing, I guess." Margaret, a student who attended the 2004 trip, said in an e-mail interview, "To me the word justice means to be free and to be fair, to get treated fairly." Two others had difficulty forming a definition. Jackie said:

> But, to put it in my own words, I mean, I don't know how to define justice. But I know that our trip was a lot about justice. To learn about the Native American culture and everything that they went through. And I guess they wanted justice for themselves. God, I don't know how to explain it. It's on the tip of my tongue, but I don't even know how to explain it. I hate it when this happens to me. I know what I want to say, but just can't say it.

A few students, such as Hannah, Adrienne and Suzy, had immediate responses. When asked to define justice, Hannah said:

> Hannah: Justice to me is righting the wrong. Not necessarily punishing people, but doing just or good for someone who has been done wrong.
>
> Amy: In what ways do you think Circle relates to that?
>
> Hannah: Cuz when you are looking for justice you normally need to seek others and you need help. You can't do it all by yourself. More than one voice is stronger than just a single one.

Hannah's insight that social justice is something that can't be done alone shows significant awareness from a seventeen-year-old. Indeed, key texts in the research discuss the importance of not fighting for social justice alone (Manglitz, Johnson-Bailey, and Cervero, 2005; Adams, Bell and Griffin, 1997; Ayers, Hunt, and Quinn, 1998; Landsman, 2001; and, Kumashiro, 2004).

Adrienne believed that justice was about helping others. She spoke of our community service project and her sense of community:

> I learned that I could make a difference. At first it was all hot and I didn't want to do it, cuz it was hard and I didn't think one person could made so much of a difference. It doesn't take that much, once you put all your effort

together to help somebody. I learned that there's no excuse, for somebody having an injustice done to them, for us not to help them, because we can make a difference.

When asking Angel Salathe about justice, she also speaks of community:

> I also believe that young people, when they come together in a Circle, are empowered, find strength, courage, and confidence not only in themselves, but one another. It then sparks a real purpose in them, one in which I have seen them [youth] come together and want to impact the communities in which they live. To "give back" to a society, in which, in many cases, has turned its back on them. This too shows the resiliency of young people, especially those "at-risk." In my eyes, community is the world around us whether that be our peer group, our school, our family, our neighborhoods or the world at large. I truly believe that the Circle process both builds and strengthens community.

For Suzy the definition of justice was more about internal processes:

> Amy: What is your definition of justice? What do you think justice is?
>
> Suzy: To feel and need security. And to feel that there's closure after something has happened. That's basically my definition of justice.
>
> Amy: What ways did Circle teach you about social justice?
>
> Suzy: It was just weird how I had never heard about some of the stuff. [Sigh] Um, I'd probably like to spread my feelings about it. It just made me feel more outgoing. That I can say this and it will be OK. Knowing that nobody will judge me because of what I said.

For Suzy, her ability to restore justice and work to correct injustices was directly tied to her feelings of confidence and self-worth. She believed that she could be a better advocate now that she had the knowledge gained through the curriculum, and the confidence to speak up. The crucial issue of confidence is something that is not often discussed openly when working with students about social justice. Facilitators and teachers often speak of safety for students involved, but we perhaps are not looking closely enough at confidence. Perhaps we can do more to raise the confidence of shy and withdrawn students such as Suzy.

Some students spoke not just of Circle but of the curriculum and how that helped them reflect on justice. Suzy specifically remembered her experience at the Wounded Knee Museum:

> Just knowing about some of the stories that we learned about. It was...most of it was really about injustice, like some of the stuff that happened at Wounded Knee or some of them I was just in awe and amazed by what had happened. And I'd never learned of it before the trip. It was just weird how I had never heard about some of the stuff.

When thinking of justice in general, teachers also felt that Circle did contribute to the social justice movement, but that it did not do so in isolation. The curriculum and community service project were key factors. Randy Bauer said:

> We promoted justice in the Wounded Knee Museum by saying, "Look at this. This is what happened and it can't be ignored." We promoted justice by introducing students to adult mentors like Dallas, the founder of *Meeting the Need*. Here's a man in a wheelchair that suffered great loss and is restoring justice to others by building a camp for people with disabilities. It's also by what we have shown. Driving through the forests and mountains and asking, "Why was the medicine wheel protected? Why should our sacred sites be protected?"

As teachers, we discussed the relationship between multicultural education, Circle, human rights education, and social justice education. We determined and wrote the following:

> It is important to read and learn about social injustices and those fighting against them. It is essential for students to know and understand the Universal Declaration of Human Rights. Using experiential learning enables students to have a hands-on connection with history, science, and nature. They can walk through the Wounded Knee Museum and see the photographs, letters, and displays. They can experience the nature that we are fighting to preserve. The next step is to introduce students to other adult mentors that walk the talk. Then it is important to reflect on this in the Circle process. The final key ingredient is to teach students to act. We did so through community service projects. After the project, we once again met in Circle to reflect and support one another, and then the cycle started again.

It is nearly impossible to separate out the impact of the core elements of our program or to really know which aspect was the most transformational because, as students wrote or spoke, many elements wove together. The evidence of the transformation, however, was apparent through their descriptions of Wounded Knee, their newfound awareness of nature, their ability to connect with each other and adults, their engagement with the curriculum, their ability to ask complex questions, and their desire to work for positive change.

I will end this chapter with Sheila's words. Eight months after the trip, she said:

> Like it really did change a lot of stuff for me. Like when I came back to school, I was more involved and I wanted to do more things, like I wanted to learn more about other people, I wanted to learn more about our country and the world. And I wanted to do things to change it too. And like, I learned from the other students that just because we're young doesn't mean we don't know anything. There are intelligent young people that have something positive they want to bring to the world too.

Afterword: Teacher as Transformative Learner

Four years have passed since our last Westward Bound program was held. During that time we faced great personal changes: Angel moved to Colorado; I had a baby girl and moved to Wisconsin; and Randy died of cancer in August of 2007. Randy's death impacted staff and students greatly and we all continue to miss him.

Prior to his death, we held a reunion Circle at my home for the 2006 students. The Circle was profoundly powerful for a number of reasons. The first reason was that Randy was very ill. His pain and fatigue was another disorienting dilemma for all of us, as we grappled with the reality that we only had a brief period of time to share with him; we were all trying to learn how to support and care for him during his time of suffering. During this Circle students and staff were able to tell Randy what he meant to us and offer gratitude to him. Randy soaked it all in and shared wisdom and insights. He provided a model of how to fight cancer with a tenacious spirit of dignity and grace. Students still speak of what they learned about life by observing this. One student said, "He could have been so bitter and become hard, but he didn't. I always think of that when I have something tough come up in my life."

Circle was also powerful because we were all able to connect again. Angel had moved to Colorado and flew back to spend time with Randy and to participate in our Circle of Reunion. Some students had graduated and were exploring new chapters in their lives, while others were still attending our alternative school. Though some of the students had stayed in touch with each other, others had not seen each other since the trip ended. At first students were nervous with each other and began hesitantly speaking. However, as soon as we sat in Circle and I began reading an opening poem, a relaxed energy filled the room. The feelings of connectedness returned and students openly spoke about what connectedness means to them. One of them said, "It's just here. As soon as we started Circle all those feelings of connection came right back. I miss it and I wish I could feel this way every day."

During the writing of the book I was able to interview five of the 2006 students in-depth again. Interviewing students during the trip, six months after the trip, and then four years after the trip revealed that the transformative learning experience had a long-lasting impact on their lives. Though each interview was held separately, when asked if anything from the program still influenced him or her, each student brought up Circle. "I'd never felt that close to people before, not even my family," said one student. "I think it made me realize that trusting people was possible."

Suzy brought up empowerment. She said that Circle enabled her to realize that her voice mattered and that other people would listen. She said that the trip had a lasting impact on her sense of self and played an important role in her fight with depression:

> I realized that I couldn't really seclude myself anymore. Like I realized that that's not really healthy. And I realized that I have to let all my feelings out when I'm feeling them. I really learned how important I really am. Because I was kind of attacking myself and feeling that everything was wrong because of me or just like wondering what if I wasn't here. Then I went on the trip and I realized that I am important and that I am an important piece. Otherwise if I weren't here it would be a lot different...that I played an important role. It showed me that people needed me. It showed me that I am important.

Margaret again stated that Circle showed her that forgiveness was possible. She also said, "I'll always remember what those nights around the campfire felt like. How easy it was to connect to other people."

Each student also stated that they think of the Westward Bound experience as their "best time in school" or their "favorite way to learn." Three of the five students said that they selected adult programs of study that specifically included hands-on learning such as cosmetology school, medical technician programs, and wildlife management. The trip enabled them to find a style of learning that they liked and they continue to look for opportunities to learn through experiences, rather than only via textbooks or lectures. "I don't think I would have even graduated without the trip," said one student. "It helped me get through those last credits because I started to like to learn again. I just wish I could've done all of school that way."

These recollections of Circle and hands-on learning were not unique to this group. Whenever I get in contact with other students informally, many repeat similar statements. So why don't more schools incorporate programs like this into each semester of learning? Is it cost? Risk? Scheduling concerns? Whatever the perceived roadblock, finding teachers who are passionate about re-engaging "at-risk" students and utilizing his or her skills through hands-on learning programs and connectedness tools, such as Circle, can bring about positive changes. I applaud the many alternative programs, charter schools, and public schools that continue to supply students with experiences outside of the traditional classroom. Programs such as Expeditionary Learning Outward Bound, for example, enable teachers to bring hands-on learning and expeditions into their classrooms and communities. Research has indicated that these programs impact at-risk learners positively, provide quality training for staff, and increase standardized test scores (Bormanet al, 2000; Killion, 1999). Providing these programs, especially for disengaged learners, is an essential component of dropout prevention and could revitalize broken systems and inspire disenfranchised teachers.

And what about the teachers? Though the book focused mainly on student transformations, Angel, Randy, and I also transformed as a result of these experiences. Angel and I spoke over the phone in 2010 and this recorded conversation revealed that the program transformed the ways that we think about quality education, our ideas about colleagues, and our sense of identity as a teacher. The questions were not preplanned, so our answers are honest and informal.

Angel first reflects on the program overall:

Angel: Any time I'm camping and have a fire, that's the first thing that I think about— how the kids were transformed. And it was transformational to me because I got to work closely with you and Randy, which, my whole teaching career I had not been able to do that until I did it with you guys, and I have not been able to do that since. That's something that I think about all the time and it helped me be a better teacher and a better person. And that's not anything that I can ever get back. You know it was what it was. And that was very spiritual for me. You know, having those experiences...just being in the presence of you and Randy and learning so much about myself. You see the kids transformed, but seeing each other transformed was just a joy.

Amy: Can you describe how you were transformed in the way that you taught?

Angel: I think it transformed me as a teacher because it opened my eyes to the knowledge that teaching doesn't have to be in a classroom. Teaching doesn't have to be word for word out of a textbook, all those things that you see in a traditional setting. Education doesn't have to be like that. The kids can learn so much and in such depth by teaching in a manner that incorporates their skills, their interests, and showing them new places and new things. And helping them understand it in a way that is applicable to their life. This is their life. They go on these journeys or expeditions and they experience stuff...I transformed from a traditional alternative teacher to somebody who knows that that's how I want to teach. I want to work together to create curriculum that is integrated with all the different areas... In my mind, that's how education should be. And I want to teach from that perspective and I want to continue until I don't teach any more. I want to teach serendipitously. That's how I transformed—from a traditional alternative teacher into somebody who was, "Let's go do this. And we will learn all day long. And all the core subject areas are integrated together—because that's how life is. Life is all subject matters together, connected in every way shape and form." That's how I want to teach. That's how I choose to teach. Now I don't talk about one subject without relating it to another. And you have to relate it to kids' lives and I felt like I didn't do that to the best of my ability prior to doing these expeditions. But now having had those experiences and seeing the impact and the outcome of the transformations on my students, now I've become the teacher that I've strived to become.

Amy: And for me, I think that I was fully teaching in the moment. And I think that teachers talk about that in terms of a classroom and we're always striving for that, but when we were out there, like every single moment was essential. Every single moment was like breathing learning. You know it was just constant. And as a teacher I was able to respond to things and be more flexible, and also be completely having the time of my life in these moments. And even when there were really hard times and we were exhausted and ready to be done, it was just this exhilarating experience. It was teaching me how to teach in the moment, which I had never completely experienced before.

Angel: Yeah, you just kind of have to roll with it. And I think it is true that there are lessons in all of it. Even during those times, when we were so exhausted and there were conflicts and you look back on it later and you can't do anything but laugh, because you learned something as a teacher as your students were learning. You know, you are like this big family and you are learning together. And I agree with you, you just roll with it and if there's an opportunity that comes up to talk in depth about fossils on the side of the road in the mountains because your brakes are smoking (laughs), you just go with it. That is a serendipitous moment. That is real life education incorporating all subject areas. It does not get any better than that.

It will forever be in my mind because it had such a spiritual impact on my life. It helped me transform as a person, a teacher, a colleague—all of these things. And you can't top that.

This thread of our conversation embodied an awareness of what Parker Palmer (1997) calls the inner landscape of a teacher's life: the three paths of intellectual, emotional, and spiritual. For Angel, Randy, and me, the program deeply touched on each path. We intellectually responded to the development of new curriculum, the sharing of ideas, and the research that influenced our decision-making. The emotional path was deeply present within each of us, due in part to the emotions that students openly shared with us. Those emotions, sometimes raw and painful, sometimes joyful and filled with bliss, ran through us and over us. We were open and responsive to our students' emotions, which left us exhausted at the end of each journey. Yet being present in those moments formed deep connections among all of us. Angel, Randy and I also worked through our own emotions, especially regarding Randy and his pain. In 2006, as we stood amidst the clouds at the Bighorn Medicine Wheel, we held each other and grieved, as we knew that it was the last trip that the three of us would share. And Angel states that the experience as a whole was "spiritual" for her. I would echo that. The trip highlighted all of the paths, creating a space for teaching in the moment.

Amy: Do you find that you compare those experiences to all others? And that you are always striving as a teacher to get back to that?

Angel: Yeah. I mean I do think that you can't top it.

Amy: Yeah, nothing else measures up.

Angel: No, it doesn't. I would like to be in a position where I could have new experiences and new expeditions. Connect with peers, connect with students.

Amy: I think that I always find myself comparing myself as a teacher to the teacher that I was in those moments. And because of the way we had it set up, because we were traveling, because we were doing multicultural education, social justice education, Circle, all of these elements it was such a fulfilling experience. I've never been, I guess "allowed," to do that again. And so it's almost as if I look longingly at that teacher who I was. I can bring those elements into my classroom, but it doesn't have the same energy. It doesn't have the same taste. It's just very different.

Angel: I agree with you...I do long to get back to teaching in an environment where I am allowed to and able to really put forth my potential as a teacher.

The fact that we felt like we were teaching to our full potential during these expeditions is significant. Though Angel and I continue to teach, and bring forward pieces of our curriculum and program into our current settings, we feel that we often face barriers within daily classroom routines. Bells, schedules, and nonintegrated content often interfere with our goal to teach students relevant topics that mirror life experiences. The "factory model" of education simply gets in our way. As soon as we feel excitement begin to build in our classrooms, the bell rings and middle and secondary students are forced to move on to a totally new subject, with new instructors, and in a new space. Angel and I thrive as educators when we perceive a student's heightened level of interest and are then able to act on it, individualize the type of instruction, and connect one student's interest to that of another student through dialogue and conversation. We agree with scholar John Abbott (2010) who states:

One of the most faulty pervasive assumptions in the Western education system is that actually children don't want to learn and that we have to force learning on them. And that undermines the whole thing from beginning to end. The assumption is that learning is quote "an unnatural activity." Really from everything that we now understand, and we didn't need the new science to tell us this, our grandparents new this, ancient people knew this. We are an inquisitive species. We love to find things out. We get bored to tears if people tell us too much. And schools are full of telling because quote "it's more economic." You can have thirty people sitting there in front of a teacher and they tell them a lot. In fact, the secret to learning is not the lecture it's the conversation...so the faulty assumption is that children don't want to learn and actually it's the exact opposite. So we have to create an education system, which feeds the inquisitiveness of children. (Abbott, 2010)

Our Westward Bound program does this, but it is only a microcosm of the types of educational policy and programmatic changes that need to occur so that all children can feel creative, integrated, relevant experiences in schools. For both of us, teaching in Westward Bound transformed us into advocates for systemic educational change. Yet we still use words such as "allowed" when discussing our role as educators. We still fear that rocking the boat could cost us our jobs in certain situations. I believe that many educators face similar challenges and are unable to create necessary change because they feel a lack of support or a sense of helplessness regarding how to maneuver through bureaucracy and political climates.

Our ideas about collegial support within educational settings were transformed as a result of our Westward Bound experiences. We moved from teachers who generally taught in isolation, to teachers who believed in the transformative power of collegial partnerships.

Amy: How did the whole program transform your ideas about colleagues?

Angel: All my experiences since then, obviously I've worked in an inner city school, was a principal for expelled kids, and now working with three adult programs, I have not found anything that would even resemble the trust, the support, the encouragement, the honoring of one's talents and abilities that I had with you and Randy. I long to have that again and that's probably one thing that will never show itself as it did. Working with colleagues in fifteen years of teaching I was closer to you and Randy during our times of expeditions that lasted three weeks to a month of every year and those relationships with you as my colleagues in that type of setting...I wish I could have that in every job. You know I long for that. And I miss it....In your classroom, you're used to working by yourself and bringing forth your area, your curriculum, and your subject matter and what we did was we fed off of each other and we really complemented each other. Even though you're an English teacher, Bauer was science and I'm social studies, there were times when the science, history, and English just blurred together. I didn't feel like there was one specific subject area that each of us was responsible for. We all brought our expertise and our life experiences to the table and were able to work together as a team that I'd never been a part of before like this. And we were able to work together to give our students the most memorable educational experience that a teacher could ever give their students.

Amy: Yeah, I think for me it transformed my idea of partnership and integrating all subject areas. It was just very comfortable. It felt very comfortable to have all of the subjects together. And part of that was that there was just this sense of huge trust that you or Randy would fill in any holes that I had. We trusted each other so much with our content areas that there was just always someone there that could add more, answer something or come up with a great question and it was just a huge level of trust and belief in each other's ability. We really strongly believe and believed that we were working with top educators that would step up and become a partner in all of that. And I think that it makes me search for that again, but it also kind of gives me hope that that is possible. Because I think that my perception of adult colleagues was kind of low before we started the trip. So it's transformed me in the sense that it has given me hope and belief that adults can work together like that. Now it's constantly looking for those doorways into any type of partnership or collegiality.

Angel also speaks of the power of our Westward Bound partnerships enabling her to be both teacher and learner:

I think another transformation for me as far as colleagues go is that on those trips and working with you both, I was a teacher and a student at the same time because I was not only teaching other people, but I was learning myself. Learning from my students, learning from you guys. I felt like specific things that you were experts at, I was learning right along with the students when you were talking or teaching. I was learning things that I didn't know before. That's one thing that you don't get in a traditional setting, even an alternative setting, when you are in a classroom by yourself. This gives you the opportunity to be a teacher and a student. If you want to talk about being lifelong learner, taking in as much as you give out…I think that's sometimes what is missing in traditional education. Teachers want to be teachers and not students and they are not really open to learning from their students or their colleagues. And that never was the case in our situation. I felt like we were constantly teaching each other and constantly learning from one another. The students were not the only ones benefitting from our expertise.

Amy: I agree with that. There was one journal entry of mine from the trip where I wrote, "I feel like a kid again, because I'm learning so much from Randy and from Angel." And I think that you are completely right that that is a huge part of the joy of this for me—I was as engaged as the kids were.

Angel: Exactly. I think that us being open to not only teaching, but also learning from one another is a total model. We didn't think about it as such, but we were totally modeling the give and take of teaching and learning in education. And I don't think the kids could be around us for that long without noticing that we were also learning from one another. When they see adults in their life whom they do trust and have respect for modeling what that can look like—that nobody is an authority figure talking down to you instead we're talking with one another in dialogue—that was modeling the kind of connections that adults and young adults can have as far as teaching and learning from one another. We were open to teaching and learning from our students and that was very obvious. And I think that made the whole experience for everybody that much greater.

Another aspect of the educational system that needs to change is that teachers need to be open to learning together and from each other. Movements across the globe, such as Dufour and Eaker's (1998) work on professional learning communities, are encouraging more teacher-teacher collaboration. Yet the success of those partnerships is often impacted by a wide variety of variables such as resistant staff, inadequate training, and whether the partnerships are assigned by administration or self-selected. Angel, Randy, and I were fortunate to experience a partnership that felt natural and was formed around similar interests and passions.

Another way in which Angel and I were transformed is tied to our feelings of connectedness, trust, and vulnerability. It was not just students who felt internal changes as a result of time spent in Circle, in nature, or with each other. We also felt shifts in our levels of openness with students.

Angel: You just appreciate the moment that you're in, you're taking it all in and growing as a person and seeing all these things. You know I think about it a lot. It has impacted me so much. I think about you guys as my colleagues and my friends, I think about the students, and when I hear from them and hear how great they are doing and that they have families of their own. It has such an impact on my life. Years later it still affects me. I sit around a fire and there's this explosion of emotion knowing that I was able to do those things with the people that was with.

Amy: I think that for me it was transformational because I think that as a teacher I dropped my guard even more. I mean as a teacher, I've always been really open and fluid in a classroom, but out there I was able to drop that emotional guard even more and just be completely raw and honest with the kids, just like they were being with us. I thought that that was really kind of a model for how I want to engage and communicate with students now.

I do think that there were also times that the roller coaster of emotions left us so exhausted that we were able to grow in the midst of that. We were able to make decisions like, "You know, I'm not going to tackle these two fighting girls right now because it's just not the time and place." But there was growth of letting go of a lot of the mental blocks that I would have up. The kids talk about that that is what they went through, but I think that we went through it as well. Even with Randy. I think about the last Circle at our house and that Randy was so emotionally available to everyone. That he could just close his eyes and kind of be open to all of the love that was in that room. It's kind of that paradox of being vulnerable with the kids, yet being comfortable and in control at the same time.

Angel: I believe that we were all able to show our emotions regardless of what they were. And just be real in the faces of these kids. If something made us sad, we cried. If something made us frustrated, we made it known. It's just being able to be emotionally open like that also models for kids that it's O.K. to show emotion and is healthy to show emotion as long as you're doing it in a positive way. And that you can have others help you with those emotions.

Amy: And they were able to see us work through those emotions. I remember when our van tire popped and I was trying to get through the stress of it. I was crouched down by the tire and I remember Clyde coming out and just kind of putting his hand on my shoulder. And then our students started seeing us problem solving and they began problem solving with us.

Angel: That's what I'm talking about. We allowed the students to be a part of it. We showed them that we're a team and a big family now.

This project has been a gift for me because it has shown me that we still are that family. As I've reconnected with our students, reflected on our journeys together, and told students about the project as it has grown, I have been amazed at our ability to continue to share, continue to support, and continue to learn together. Though four years have passed these experiences and the transformations that we all went through continue to impact each of us in unique personal ways.

But what does this study mean for education? This research is an example of how students and staff can be re-engaged with learning. It provides a model for teachers and administrators showing how connectedness can be promoted through Circle. Though Circle takes time, it is a tool that can be used to foster connectedness, assess student knowledge and skill, and provide a space for students to feel empowered. The study also shows that human rights, service learning and multicultural education can inspire learners to interact with their communities in a new way. Out of the five students interviewed in 2010 all still actively volunteer in their community in some capacity. Lastly, the study shows that transformative learning can happen with older adolescents.

The project leaves me with many questions, the most prevalent being, "What is stopping schools from making innovative educational change?" The number of disengaged learners grows much faster than our rate of innovation in the world of education. What can we do to speed up the reform process? How can small programs like this influence educational policy? Why aren't more classroom teachers researching? What can we do to bring more student voices into educational research and reform? How can we prepare secondary education teachers to facilitate and foster transformative learning?

My hope is that this book provides teachers and administrators insights into programmatic changes within their daily schedules, especially regarding our most disengaged learners. I do believe that all learners can succeed if provided with interesting, relevant, engaging, hands-on learning experiences in a safe, nurturing environment. In addition, I hope that it provides teachers who are currently running similar programs with inspiration to conduct research studies of their own, so that successful programs can serve as models for future innovation.

References

Abbott, J. (2010). "Faulty assumptions of western education: An interview with John Abbott." Retrieved September 19, 2010, from http://www.youtube.com/watch?v=bIwoiVWg84E&feature=related

Adams, M. (1997). Pedagogical frameworks for social justice education. In M. Adams, L. A. Bell, & P. Griffin (Eds.) (1997). *Teaching for diversity and social justice: A sourcebook.* New York: Routledge.

Adams, M., Bell, L. A., & Griffin, P. (Eds.) (1997). *Teaching for diversity and social justice: A sourcebook.* New York: Routledge.

Ainley, M. (2006). Connecting with learning: Motivation, affect and cognition in interest processes. *Educational Psychology Review*, 18, 391–405.

Alexie, S. (1992). *The Business of Fancy Dancing.* Brooklyn, NY: Hanging Loose Press.

Artelt, C. (2005). Cross-cultural approaches to measuring motivation. *Educational Assessment*, 10 (3), 231–255.

Au, W. (2009). The "building tasks" of critical history: Structuring social studies for social justice. *Social Science Research & Practice*, 4 (2), 24–35. Retrieved on August 5, 2010, from http://www.socstrp.org/issues/PDF/4.2.2pdf

Augustine, D. K., Gruber, K. D., & Hanson, L. R. (December1989/January 1990). Cooperation works. *Educational Leadership*, 4–7.

Ayers, W., Hunt, J. A., Quinn, T. (Eds.). (1998). Teaching for Social Justice: A Democracy and Education Reader. New York, NY: The New Press.

Baldwin, C. (1994). *Calling the circle: The first and future culture.* New York: Bantam Doubleday Dell.

Baldwin, C. (2005). *Storycatcher: Making sense of our lives through the power and practice of story.* Novato, CA: New World Library.

Banks, C. A. M., & Banks, J. A. (1995). Equity Pedagogy: An Essential Component of Multicultural Education. *Theory into Practice*, 34 (3), 151–158.

Banks, J. A. (1988). *Multiethnic education: Theory and practice.* 2nd edition. Boston: Allyn and Bacon.

Banks, J. A. (1997). Multicultural Education: Characteristics and Goals. In J. A. Banks & C. A. M. Banks, (Eds.). *Multicultural Education: Issues and Perspectives* (3rd ed., pp. 3–31). Boston: Allyn and Bacon.

Banks, J. A. (2004). Multicultural education: Characteristics and goals. In J. A. Banks and C. A. Mcgee Banks (Eds.) *Multicultural education: Issues and perspectives* (5th edition). Hoboken, NJ: John Wiley and Sons.

Baumgartner, L. M. (2002). Living and learning with HIV/AIDS: Transformational tales continued. *Adult Education Quarterly*, 53, 44–70.

Beck, M., & Malley, J. (1998). A pedagogy of belonging. *Reclaiming Youth and Children*, 7, 133–135.

Belenky, M., & Stanton, A. (2000). Inequality, development, and connected knowing. In J. Mezirow (Ed.), *Learning as Transformation* (pp. 71–102). San Francisco, CA: Jossey-Bass.

Berman, D., & Davis-Berman, J. (1995). *Outdoor education and troubled youth.* Charleston, WV. (ERIC Document Reproduction Service No. ED385425). Retrieved July 30, 2010, from EBSCOHost ERIC database

Bernard, B. (2004). Turnaround teachers and schools. In B. Williams (Ed.), *Closing the Achievement Gap: A vision for changing beliefs and practices* (2nd edition), p. 115–137. Alexandria, VA: ASCD.

Bigelow, B. (1990). Inside the classroom: Social vision and critical pedagogy. *Teachers College Record,* 91, 437–448.

Bigelow, B., & Peterson, B. (2002). *Rethinking globalization: Teaching for justice in an unjust world.* Milwaukee: Rethinking schools.

Blum, R., & Libbey, H. (2004). Executive summary. *Journal of School Health,* 74, 231–232.

Borman, J. D., Hewes, G. M., Overman, L. T., & Brown, S. (2002). *Comprehensive school reform and student achievement: A meta-analysis.* Center for Research on the Education of Students Placed At Risk. Retrieved September 11, 2010, from http://elschools.org/about-us/research-el

Box, J. A., & Little, D. C. (2003). Cooperative small-group instruction combined with advanced organizers and their relationship to self-concept and social studies achievement of elementary school students. *Journal of Instructional Psychology,* 30 (4), 285–287.

Boyes-Watson, C. (2002). *The journey of circles at ROCA.* Report on the Period July 2001–June 30, 2002. The Center for Restorative Justice at Suffolk University. Retrieved October 8, 2006, from http://www.rocainc.org/pdf/circle.pdf

Boyes-Watson, C. (2005). Seeds of change: Using peacemaking circles to build a village for every child. *Child Welfare,* 84, 191–208.

Boyes-Watson, C. (2008). *Peacemaking circles & urban youth: Bringing justice home.* St. Paul, MN: Living Justice Press.

Brewster, C. & Fager, J. (2000, October). *Increasing student engagement and motivation: from time-on-task to homework.* Portland, Oregon: Northwest Regional Educational Laboratory.

Bridgeland, J. M.; Dilulio J. J., Jr., & Morison, K. B. (2006). *The silent epidemic: Perspectives of high school dropouts.* Washington, D.C.: Civic Enterprises, LLC. Retrieved on August 5, 2010, from http://www.civicenterprises.net/pdfs/thesilentepidemic3-06.pdf

Brockman, N. C. (1998). *Encyclopedia of sacred places.* New York: Oxford University Press, 24–25.

Brookfield, S. D. (1990). *The skillful teacher.* San Fransisco: Jossey-Bass.

Brown, D. (1998). *Bury my heart at wounded knee: An Indian history of the American west.* New York: Vintage.

Cassidy, W., & Bates, A. (2005). "Drop-outs" and "push-outs": Finding hope at a school that actualizes the ethic of care. *American Journal of Education,* 112, 66–102.

Catalano, R., Haggerty, K., Oesterle, S., Fleming, C., Hawkins, D. (2004). The importance of bonding to school for healthy development: Findings from the social development research group. *Journal of School Health,* 74, 252–261.

Chavez, A. F., & Guido-DiBrito, F. (1999). Racial and ethnic identity and development. *New Directions for Adult and Continuing Education*, 84 (Winter).

Clark, M. (2008). Celebrating disorienting dilemmas: Reflections from the rear view mirror [Electronic version]. *Adult learning*, 19, 47–49.

Claus, J., & Ogden, C. (2004). An empowering, transformative approach to service. In *Service learning for youth empowerment and social change*. Adolescent Cultures, School & Society Series, V. 5, pp. 69–94. New York: Peter Lang Publishing.

Coates, R., Umbreit, M., & Vos, B. (2003). Restorative justice circles: An exploratory study. *Contemporary Justice Review*, 6, 265–278.

Collatos, A., & Morrell, E. (2003). Apprenticing urban youth as critical researchers: Implications for school reform. In B. Rubin and E. Silva (Eds.), *Critical Voices in School Reform: Students Living Through Change*. New York : Routledge/ Falmer.

Collay, M., Dunlap, D., Enloe, W., Gagnon, G., Jr. (1998). *Learning circles: Creating conditions for professional development*. Thousand Oaks, CA: Corwin Press, Inc.

Committee on Increasing High School Students' Engagement and Motivation to Learn, & National Research Council. (2003). *Engaging schools: Fostering high school students' motivation to learn*. Washington, D.C.: National Academies Press.

Couch, G., & Hall, M. (1992). Perspectives: The use in experiential education of ceremonies and rituals from Native American cultures. *The Journal of Experiential Education*, 15, 51–55.

Cranton, P. (2006). *Understanding and promoting transformative learning (2ⁿᵈ edition)*. San Francisco, CA: Jossey-Bass.

Cross, R. (2002). The effects of an adventure education program on perceptions of alienation and personal control among at-risk adolescents. *The Journal of Experiential Education*, 25, 247–254.

Cummins, J. (1986). Empowering minority students: A framework for intervention. *Harvard Educational Review*, 56, 18–36.

Cushner, K. (2003). *Human diversity in action: Developing multicultural competencies for the classroom*. New York: McGraw-Hill.

D'Amato, L. G., & Krasny, M.E., (2009). *Outdoor adventure education: Applying transformative learning theory in addressing instrumental and emancipatory EE goals*. Manuscript submitted for publication.

Delpit, L. (1995). *Other people's children: Cultural conflict in the classroom*. New York: The New Press.

Deschenes, S., Tyack, D., & Cuban, L. (2001). Mismatch: Historical perspectives on schools and students who don't fit them. *Teachers College Record*, 103, 525–547. Retrieved December, 16, 2006, from http://www.tcrecord.org/PrintContent.asp?ContentID=10773

Dirkx, J. (1998). Transformative learning theory in the practice of adult education: An overview. *PAACE Journal of Lifelong Learning*, 7, 1–14.

Dotson, J. (2001). Cooperative learning structures can increase student achievement. *Kagan Online Magazine*, Winter 2001. Retrieved July 15, 2010, from http://www.kaganonline.com/free_articles/research_and_rationale/increase_achi evement.php

Dufour, R., & Eaker, R. (1998). Professional learning communities at work: Best practices for enhancing student achievement. Bloomington: Solution Tree.

Dynarski, M., & Wood, R. (1997). *Helping high-risk youth: Results from the Alternative Schools Demonstration Program.* Princeton, NJ: Mathematica Policy Research.

Erdrich, L. (2003). *Original fire: New and selected poems.* New York: Harper Collins.

Facing History and Ourselves 2009 Annual Report (2009). Retrieved from http://www.facinghistory.org/sites/facinghistory.org/files/AnnualReport2009/index.html

Flavin, M. (1996). *Kurt Hahn's school and legacy: To discover you can be more and do more than you believed.* Wilmington, DE: Middle Atlantic Press.

Flowers, N. (Ed.) (1997). *Human rights here and now.* University of Minnesota: Human Rights Resource Center. Retrieved August 11, 2010, from http://www1.umn.edu/humanrts/edumat/hreduseries/hereandnow/Intro/acknowledgements.htm

Franklin, C., Streeter, C. L., Kim, J. S., & Tripodi, S. J. (2007). The effectiveness of a solution-focused, public alternative school for dropout prevention and retrieval. *Children & Schools, 29* (30), 133–144.

Freire, P. (1970). *Pedagogy of the oppressed.* New York, NY: Continuum.

Gambrell, L. B. (2001). What we know about motivation to read. In R.F. Flippo, *Reading Researchers in Search of Common Ground* (pp. 129–143). Newark, Delaware: International Reading Association.

Garrett, J. T., & Garrett, M. W. (1994). The path of good medicine: Understanding and counseling Native American Indians. *Journal of Multicultural Counseling and Development, 22* (3), 133–144.

Garst, B., Scheider, I., & Baker, D. (2001). Outdoor adventure program participation impacts on adolescent self-perception. The Journal of Experiential Education, 24, 41-49.

Gay, G. (2000). *Culturally responsive teaching: Theory, research, and practice.* New York: Teachers College Press.

Ghosh, R., & Abdi, A. A. (2004). *Education and the politics of difference: Canadian perspectives.* Toronto: Canadian Scholars Press.

Giroux, H. A. (1994). Doing cultural studies: Youth and the challenge of pedagogy [Electronic version]. *Harvard Educational Review,* 64 (3), 278–308. Retrieved August 11, 2010, from http://www.henryagiroux.com/online_articles/doing_cultural.htm

Gomez, R. A. (1991). *Teaching with a multicultural perspective.* Urbana, IL: ERIC clearinghouse on elementary and early childhood education. (ERIC Document Reproduction Service No. ED339548). Retrieved August 4, 2010, from http://www.ericdigests.org/1992-5/perspective.htm

Gorski, P. (2009). Cognitive dissonance as a strategy in social justice teaching. *Multicultural Education,* Fall.

Gostev, M., & Weis, F. M. (2007). Firsthand nature. *Science and Children,* 44(8), 48–51.

Greenwood, J. (2005). The circle process: A path for restorative dialogue. *The Center for Restorative Justice and Peacemaking*. University of Minnesota. Retrieved October, 14, 2006, from http://rjp.umn.edu/img/assets/13522/The_Circle_Process.pdf

Guthrie, J. T., Wigfield, A. L., Humenick, N. M., Perencevich, K. C., Taboada, A., & Barbosa, P. (2006). Influences of stimulating tasks on reading motivation and comprehension. *The Journal of Educational Research*, 99 (4), 232–245.

Hahn, K. (1957). *Outward Bound*. New York: World Books.

Hamilton, S., & Fenzel, M. (1988). The impact of volunteer experience on adolescent social development. *Journal of Adolescent Research*, 3: 65–80.

Harada, V., & Yoshina, J. (2004). Moving from rote to inquiry: Creating learning that counts. *Library Media Connection*, 23 (2), 22–25.

Harjo, J. (2004). *How we became human: New and selected poems 1975–2001*. New York: W.W. Norton & Company.

Hazen-Hammond, S. (1999) Spider woman's web: Traditional Native American tales about women's power. New York: Perigree.

Helms, J. E. (1984). Toward a theoretical explanation of the effects of race on counseling: A black and white model. *The Counseling Psychologist*, 12, 153–165.

Helms, J.E., & Carter, R. T. (1990*).* Development of the White Racial Identity Attitude Inventory. In J.E. Helms (Ed.), *Black and White racial identity: Theory, research, and practice* (pp. 67–80). Westport, CT Greenwood.

Helms, J.E. (1997). Toward a model of White racial identity development (pp. 207–224). In P. G. Altbach, K. Arnold, & I. Carreiro King (Ed.), *College student development and academic life: Psychological, intellectual, social and moral issues*. New York: Taylor and Francis. Retrieved August 4, 2010, from http://books.google.com/books?lr=&id=xsO1IlWMEOAC&dq=helms+white+identity+model&q=

Herdman, P. (1994). When the wilderness becomes a classroom. *Educational Leadership*, 52, 15–19.

Heusman, S., & Moenich, D. (2003) Achievement still on the rise at Catalina Ventura High School. *Kagan Online Magazine*, Summer 2003. Retrieved July 15, 2010, from http://www.kaganonline.com/free_articles/research_and_rationale/increase_achievement.php

Hill, E. (2005). *Building resiliency among adolescents with substance abuse problems*. Paper presented at the 32nd Annual International Conference of the Association for Experiential Education, November 4–7, 2004. Norfolk, Virginia.

Holmes, K. L. (Ed.). (1995). *Covered wagon women, volume 1: Diaries and letters from the western trails*. Winnepeg, MB, Canada: Bison Books.

Hopkins, B. (2002). Restorative justice in schools [Electronic version]. *Support for Learning*, 17, 3, 144–149.

Horton, M. (1998). *The Long Haul: Autobiography*. New York: Teachers College Press.

Hughes, L. (1990). *Selected poems of Langston Hughes*. New York, NY: Vintage.

Human Rights Here and Now (1998). Ed. Flowers, N. Human Rights Educators' Network. USA: Amnesty International. Retrieved August 4, 2010, from University of

Minnesota   http://www1.umn.edu/humanrts/edumat/hreduseries/hereandnow/
Default.htm

Itin, C. (1999). Reasserting the philosophy of experiential education as a vehicle for
change in the 21st century. *The Journal of Experiential Education*, 22, 91.

Jalongo, M. R. (2007). Beyond benchmarks and scores: Reasserting the role of motivation and interest in children's academic achievement [Electronic version]. *Childhood Education*, 83 (6), 395–407.

Jennings, G. (2003). An exploration of meaningful participation and caring relationships
as contexts for school engagement. *The California School Psychologist*, 8, 43–52.

Joplin, L. (1995). On defining experiential education. In Warren, Sakofs, & Hunt Jr.
(Eds.), *The theory of experiential education*. Boulder, CO: Association for Experiential Education.

Kagan, S. (1994). *Kagan Cooperative Learning*.

Kailin, J. (2002). *Antiracist education: From theory to practice*. Lanham, MD: Rowman &
Littlefield Publishers Inc.

Killion, J. (1999). *What works in the middle: Results-based staff development*. Dallas, TX:
The National Staff Development Council. Retrieved September 11, 2010, from
http://www.nsdc.org/midbook/index.html

Klem, A., & Connell, J. (2004). Relationships matter: Linking teacher support to stu-
dent engagement and achievement. *Journal of School Heath*, 74, 262–273. Retrieved
December 9, 2006, from http://www.ojjdp.ncjrs.gov/truancy/pdf/Jour School-
HealthSept2004.pdf

Kneller, G. (1971). *Foundations of education*. Hoboken, NJ: John Wiley & Sons, Inc.

Kolb, D. (1984). *Experiential learning: Experience as the source of learning and development*.
Englewood Cliffs, NJ: Prentice Hall P T R.

Kraft, D., & Sakofs, M. (Eds.). (1988). *The theory of experiential education*. Boulder, CO:
Association for Experiential Education.

Kumashiro, K. (2001). "Posts" perspectives on anti-oppressive education in social
studies, English, mathematics, and science classrooms. *Educational Researcher*, 30:
3–12.

Kumashiro, K. (2004). *Against common sense: Teaching and learning toward social justice*.
New York: Routledge.

Ladson-Billings, G. (1994). *The dreamkeepers: Successful teachers of African American
children*. San Francisco, CA: Jossey-Bass.

Ladson-Billings, G., & Tate, W. (1995). Toward a critical race theory in education.
Teachers College Record, 97, (1), p. 47–68 http://www.tcrecord.org ID Number:
1410, Date Accessed: 4/25/2010 11:39:02 AM

Landsman, J. (2001). *A white teacher talks about race*. Lanham, MD: The Scarecrow
Press.

Lewis, G. (2002). *Teaching and learning in circle*. Paper presented at the Third International Conference on Conferencing, Circles and other Restorative Practices, Minneapolis, MN. Retrieved October 8, 2006, from http://www.campus-
adr.org/CMHER/ReportArticles/Edition3_2/Lewis3_2a.html

Libbey, H. (2004). Measuring student relationships to school: Attachment, bonding, connectedness, and engagement. *Journal of School Health*, 74, 274–283. Retrieved December 1, 2007, from http://www.ojjdp.ncjrs.gov/truancy/pdf/JourSchool HealthSept2004.pdf

Loewen, J. W. (2010). *Teaching what really happened: How to avoid the tyranny of textbooks & get students excited about doing history* (Multicultural education series). New York: Teachers College Press.

Louv, R. (2005). *Last child in the woods: Saving our children from nature-deficit disorder.* Chapel Hill, NC: Algonquin Books.

Luchetti, C. (2001). *Women of the west.* New York: W.W. Norton and Company.

Lumsden, L. (1999). *Student motivation: Cultivating a love of learning* [Electronic copy]. University of Oregon: ERIC Publications.

Manglitz, E., Johnson-Bailey, J., & Cervero, R. (2005). Struggles of hope: How white adult educators challenge racism. *Teachers College Record*, 107 (6), 1245–1274.

Marshall, J. M., III (2004). *The journey of crazy horse: A Lakota history.* New York: Penguin.

Marshall, J. M., III (2001). *The Lakota way: Stories and lessons for living.* New York: Penguin Compass.

Maxwell, B. (2008). Justifying educational acquaintance with the moral horrors of history on psycho-social grounds: "Facing history and ourselves" in critical perspective. *Ethics and Education*, 3, 1: 75–85.

McDevitt, T., & Ormrod, J. (2004). *Child development: Educating and working with children and adolescents* (2nd ed.). Upper Saddle River, NJ: Pearson Education.

McIntosh, P. (1988). *White Privilege and Male Privilege: A personal account of coming to see correspondences through work in women's studies.* Working Paper #189. Wellesley, MA: Wellesley College Center for Research on Women.

McNeely, C., Nonnemaker, J., & Blum, R. (2002). Promoting school connectedness: Evidence from the national longitudinal study of adolescent health. *Journal of School Health*, 72, 138–146.

Mezirow, J. (1978). *Education for perspective transformation: Women's re-entry programs in community colleges.* New York: Teacher's College, Columbia University.

Mezirow, J. (1991). *Transformative dimensions of adult learning.* San Francisco: Jossey-Bass.

Mezirow, J. (2000). Learning to think like an adult: Core concepts of transformation theory. In J. Mezirow (Ed.), *Learning as Transformation* (pp. 3–33). San Fransisco: Jossey-Bass.

Mezirow, J. (2009). Transformative learning theory. In J. Mezirow & E. W. Taylor (Eds.), *Transformative learning in practice: Insights from community, workplace, and higher education.* San Francisco: Jossey-Bass.

Minnesota Department of Education, (2004). 2004 MN student survey statewide tables. Retrieved December 9, 2006, from MN Department of Education Web site: http://education.state.mn.us/mde/static/002038.pdf, p. 13.

Mirsky, L. (2003) *Restorative practices impact public schools in Minnesota: An interview with Nancy Riestenberg of the Minnesota department of children families and learning.* Retrieved August 10, 2010, from International Institute for Restorative Practices website: http://www.iirp.org/article_detail.php?article_id=NDM1

Momaday, N. S. (2000). *In the bear's house.* New York: St. Martin Griffin.

Moore, R. C. (1997). The need for nature: A childhood right. *Social Justice,* 24, 203–220.

Moua, M. N. (2002). *Bamboo among the oaks: Contemporary writing by Hmong Americans.* St. Paul: Minnesota Historical Society Press.

Murray, C. (2002). Supportive teacher-student relationships: Promoting the social and emotional health of early adolescents with high incidence disabilities. *Childhood Education,* 78 (5), 285.

Neil, J., & Richards, G. (1998). Does outdoor education really work?: A summary of recent meta-analyses. *Australian Journal of Outdoor Education,* 3.

Nelson, A. (2009). Storytelling and transformational learning. In Fisher-Yoshida, Geller, and Schapiro (Eds.), *Innovations in transformative learning* (pp. 207–221). New York: Peter Lang.

Nieto, S. (1992). *Affirming diversity: The sociopolitical context of multicultural education.* White Plains, NY: Longman Publishing Group.

Noddings, N. (1992). *The challenge to care in schools: An alternative approach to education.* New York: Teachers College Press.

Noddings, N. (1995). Teaching themes of care. *Phi Delta Kappan,* 76, 675–679.

Nohl, A. M. (2009). Spontaneous action and transformative learning: Empirical investigations and pragmatist reflections. *Educational Philosophy and Theory,* 41, (3), 2009. Retrieved August 5, 2010 from Academic Search Premier access number 39772398.

North, C. E. (2008). What is all this talk about "social justice"? Mapping the terrain of education's latest catchphrase. *Teachers College Record,* 110, 1182–1206.

O'Brien, M. B. (1999). *Toward the setting sun: Pioneer girls traveling the overland trails.* Helena, MT: TwoDot.

Oliver, H. (1995). Influence of motivational factors on performance. *Journal of Instructional Psychology,* 22 (1), 45–50.

O'Sullivan, E. (1999). *Transformative learning: Educational vision for the 21st century.* New York: St Martin's Press.

O'Sullivan, E. (2002). The project and vision of transformative education: Integral transformative learning. In E. O'Sullivan, A. Morrell, & M. A. O'Connor (Eds.), *Expanding the boundaries of transformative learning: Essays on theory and praxis.* New York: Palgrave.

Palmer, J. (1998). *Environmental education in the 21st century: Theory, practice, progress and promise.* London, England: Routledge.

Palmer, P. (1997). The heart of a teacher. *Change Magazine,* 29, 14–21.

Park, S. C. (2008). *Teachers' perceptions of teaching for social justice.* Unpublished doctoral dissertation, Ohio State University. Retrieved August 10, 2010, from http://etd.ohiolink.edu/sendpdf.cgi/Park%20Sung%20Choon.pdf?osu1211568529

Patton, M. Q. (2002). *Qualitative evaluation and research methods* (2nd edition). Newbury Park, London, New Delhi: Sage Publications.

Perez, S. (2000). An ethic of caring in teaching culturally diverse students. *Education, 121*, 102–106.

Phinney, J. (1990). Ethnic identity in adolescents and adults: Review of research. *Psychological Bulletin, 108* (3), 499–514. (ERIC Document Reproduction Service No. ED310193)

Pianta, R. C. (1999). Enhancing relationships between children and teachers. Washington, D. C.: American Psychological Association.

Pomeroy, E. (1999). The teacher-student relationship in secondary school: Insights from excluded students. *Brittish Journal of Sociology of Education, 20*, 465–482. Retrieved January, 1, 2007, from http://links.jstor.org/sici?sici=01425692%28199912%2920%3A4%3C465%3ATTRISS%3E2.0.CO%3B2-U

Powers, K. (2005). Promoting school achievement among American Indian students throughout the school years [Electronic version]. *Childhood Education.* Retrieved August 10, 2010, from http://www.thefreelibrary.com/Promoting+school+achievement+among+American+Indian+students..-a0136648569

Pranis, K. (2005). *The little book of circle processes.* Intercourse, PA: Good Books.

Pranis, K. (2004). Restorative justice in Minnesota and the US: Implementation and outcomes. Visiting Experts' Papers, 123rd International Senior Seminar, Resource Material Series No. 63, pp. 124–135. Retrieved December 26, 2006, from http://www.unafei.or.jp/english/pdf/PDF_rms/no63/ch13.pdf

Pranis, K., Stuart, B., & Wedge, M. (2003). *Peacemaking circles: From crime to community.* St. Paul, MN: Living Justice Press.

Rauner, D. (2000). *"They still pick me up when I fall."* Chichester: Columbia University Press.

Reardon, B. (1995). *Educating for human dignity: Learning about rights and responsibilities.* Philadelphia: University of Pennsylvania Press.

Reardon, B. (1997). Diagnosing intolerance and describing tolerance. In *Tolerance: threshold of peace, Unit 1.* Paris: UNESCO.

Riestenberg, N. (2003). Restorative Schools Grants Final Report. Retrieved December 9, 2006, from Minnesota Department of Education Web site: http://education.state.mn.us/mde/static/002676.pdf

Rodríguez, L. (2005). *My nature is hunger: New and selected poems 1989–2004.* Williamantic, CT: Curbstone Books.

Rourke, B. (2001, Spring). Restorative justice through the eyes of a high school assistant principal. *Restorative Justice in Action: 2. Special School Edition.* Denver: Colorado Forum on Community and Restorative Justice.Restorative. Retrieved October 3, 2006, from http://www.restorativejustice.org/articlesdb/articles/4176

Rugen, L. & Hartl, S. (1994). The lessons of learning expeditions. *Educational Leadership, 51*, 20–23.

Rugutt, R., & Chemosit, C. (2009). What motivates students to learn? Contribution of student-to-student relations, student-faculty interaction and critical thinking skills. *Educational Research Quarterly*, 32, 16.

Rutter, R. A., and Newmann, F. M. (1989). The potential of community service to enhance civic responsibility. *Social Education*, 53, 371–374.

Satir, V. (2003). Making contact. In S. M. Intrator & M. Scribner (Eds.), *Teaching with fire: Poetry that sustains the courage to teach*. San Fransisco: Jossey-Bass.

Sharpe, S. (1998). *Restorative justice: A vision for healing and change*. Edmonton, AB, Canada: Victim Offender Mediation Society.

Slavin, R. E., Karweit, N. L., Madden, N. A. (1989). *Effective programs for students at risk*. Boston: Allyn & Bacon.

Sleeter, C. (1996). *Multicultural education as social activism*. Albany: State University of New York Press.

Smith, T. E., Roland, C. C., Havens, M. D., Hoyt, J. A. (1992). *The theory and practice of challenge education*. Dubuque, IA: Kendall/Hunt Publishing Company.

Smolleck, L. (2008). Green teaching: The impact of no child left inside. *Teachers College Record*, October 07.

Smyth, J. (2010). Adolescent engagement, connectedness and dropping out of school. In J. DeVitis and L. Irwin-DeVitis (Eds.), *Adolescent education* (pp. 195–207). New York: Peter Lang.

Solórzano, D. G., & Yosso, T. J. (2002). Critical race methodology: Counter-storytelling as an analytical framework for education research. *Qualitative Inquiry*, 8, 23–44.

Taylor, E. W. (2000). Analyzing research on transformative learning theory. In J. Mezirow (Ed.), *Learning as transformation* (pp. 3–33). San Fransisco: Jossey Bass.

Taylor, E. W. (2009). Fostering transformative learning. In J. Mezirow, & E. Taylor (Eds.), *Transformative learning in practice* (pp. 3–17). San Fransisco: Jossey-Bass.

Te Riele, K. (2006). Schooling practices for marginalized students—practice-with-hope. *International Journal of Inclusive Education*, 10, 59–74.

Tibbits, F. (2005). Transformative learning and human rights education: Taking a closer look. *Intercultural Education*, 16, (2), 107–113.

Ukpokodu, O. (2009). Pedagogies that foster transformative learning in a multicultural education course: A reflection. *Journal of Praxis in Multicultural Education*, 4, (1).

Umbreit, M. (2003). *Talking circles*. Minneapolis, MN: The Center for http://rjp.umn.edu/img/assets/13522/Talking_Circles.pdf

UNICEF/UNESCO. (2007). A human rights-based approach to education for all. UNICEF. Retrieved August 11, 2010, from http://www.unicef.org/publications/index_42104.html

Valdez, J. (2002). Teaching multicultural diversity: Process, courage, and transformative learning. *Academic Exchange Quarterly*, December 22.

Varnham, S. (2005). Seeing things differently: Restorative justice and school discipline. *Education and the Law*, 17, 87–104.

Villegas, A. M., & Lucas, T. (2007). The culturally responsive teacher. *Educational Leadership*, 64, 28-33.

Walker, A. (2003). *A poem traveled down my arm: Poems and drawings*. New York: Random House.

Walker, L. (2001). Beyond policy: Conferencing on student misbehavior. *Principal Leadership*, 1, 7. Retrieved October 3, 2006, from http://www.lorennwalker.com/articles/student_article.html

Warner, C., & Kirby, B. (2010). *Transformational learning: Improving the adult learner experience in short term study abroad programs*. Paper presented at 25th International Conference on Improving University Teaching, Washington, DC. Retrieved July 31, 2010, from http://www.iutconference.org/papers/Expanding CulturalAttunementInAShrinkingWorld/Warner_Kirby.pdf

Washington State Institute for Public Policy. (June 2009). *What works? Targeted truancy and dropout programs in middle and high school*. Olympia, WA: Author. Retrieved August 11, 2010, from http://www.wsipp.wa.gov/rptfiles/09-06-2201.pdf

Wearmouth, J. (2007). Restorative justice in schools: A New Zealand example. *Educational Research*, 49, 37–49.

Wentzel, K., & Caldwell, K. (1997). Friendships, peer acceptance and group membership: Relations to academic achievement in middle school. *Child Development*, 68, 1198–1209.

Whitlock, J. (2006). Youth perceptions of life at school: Contextual correlates of school connectedness in adolescence. *Applied Developmental Science*, 10, 1, 13–29.

Williams, M., Cross D., Hong J., Aultman L., Osborn J., & Schutz P. (2008). There are no emotions in math: How teachers approach emotions in the classroom. *Teachers College Record*, 110, (8), 1574–1610. Retrieved April, 23, 2010, from http://www.tcrecord.org ID Number: 15153.

Wingspread Conference, (2004). Wingspread declaration on school connectedness. *Journal of School Health*. 74, 233–234.

Woolworth, A. R. (Ed.). (2003). *Santee Dakota Indian legends: Tales of the Santee Dakota Nation (volume 2)*. St. Paul, MN: Prairie Smoke Press.

Yates, M., & Youniss, J. (2004). Promoting identity development: Ten ideas for school-based service-learning programs. *Service learning for youth empowerment and social change*. Adolescent Cultures, School & Society Series, V. 5, p. 43–67. New York: Peter Lang Publishing.

Yinger, J. M. (1976). Ethnicity in complex societies. In L. A. Coser and O. N. Larsen (Eds.), *The uses of controversy in sociology*. New York: Free Press.

Zehr, H. (2002). *The Little Book of Restorative Justice*. Intercourse, PA: Good Books.

Zirkel, S. (2008). The influence of multicultural educational practices on student outcomes and intergroup relations. *Teachers College Record*, 110, 6, 1182–1206. http://www.tcrecord.org. ID Number 15043, Date Accessed: 2/21/2010.

Zweig, J. (2003). Vulnerable youth: Identifying their need for alternative educational settings. The Urban Institute: Washington, D.C. (PB 410828). Retrieved October 24, 2006, from http://www.urban.org/url.cfm?ID=410828.

Index

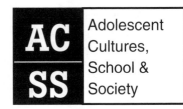

Adolescent Cultures, School & Society

Joseph L. DeVitis & Linda Irwin-DeVitis
GENERAL EDITORS

As schools struggle to redefine and restructure themselves, they need to be cognizant of the new realities of adolescents. Thus, this series of monographs and textbooks is committed to depicting the variety of adolescent cultures that exist in today's post-industrial societies. It is intended to be a primarily qualitative research, practice, and policy series devoted to contextual interpretation and analysis that encompasses a broad range of interdisciplinary critique. In addition, this series will seek to provide a pragmatic, pro-active response to the current backlash of conservatism that continues to dominate political discourse, practice, and policy. This series seeks to address issues of curriculum theory and practice; multicultural education; aggression and violence; the media and arts; school dropouts; homeless and runaway youth; alienated youth; at-risk adolescent populations; family structures and parental involvement; and race, ethnicity, class, and gender studies.

Send proposals and manuscripts to the general editors at:
Joseph L. DeVitis & Linda Irwin-DeVitis
Darden College of Education
Old Dominion University
Norfolk, VA 23503

To order other books in this series, please contact our Customer Service Department at:
(800) 770-LANG (within the U.S.)
(212) 647-7706 (outside the U.S.)
(212) 647-7707 FAX

or browse online by series at:
WWW.PETERLANG.COM